D.H. Lawrence

a collection of criticism edited by Leo Hamalian

McGraw-Hill Book Company

New York • St. Louis • San Francisco • London • Düsseldorf
Kuala Lumpur • Mexico • Montreal • Panama • São Paulo
Sydney • Toronto • Johannesburg • New Delhi • Singapore

"Reductive Energy in *The Rainbow*" pages 45–69 from *The River of Dissolution* by Colin Clarke, used by permission of Barnes & Noble, division of Harper & Row Publishers, Inc.

123456789MUMU79876543

Library of Congress Cataloging in Publication Data

Hamalian, Leo, comp.

D. H. Lawrence; a collection of criticism

(Contemporary studies in literature)

CONTENTS: Hamalian, L. Introduction.—Lawrence, D. H. Autobiography.—Lawrence, F. D. H. Lawrence, the failure. —[Etc.]
  1. Lawrence, David Herbert, 1885–1930—Addresses, essays, lectures.
PR6023.A93Z6312   823'.9'12   73-5502
ISBN 0-07-025690-X

Contents

Leo Hamalian

Introduction

In one of his *Letters to a Young Writer,* Rainer Maria Rilke declares: "Works of art are of infinite loneliness and with nothing to be so little reached as with criticism. Only love can grasp and hold and fairly judge them." No body of criticism better illustrates Rilke's meaning than the history of Lawrence criticism.

During most of Lawrence's creative career, few critics were tuned into his novels, stories, poetry, plays, criticism, and "pollyanalytics." Like William Blake, Lawrence had to endure an age that undervalued his craft, misunderstood his meaning, or rejected his vision. For instance, when his final major novel, *Lady Chatterley's Lover,* appeared in England, Scotland Yard was called upon to suppress what his countrymen called "monstrous and horrible, . . . a landmark in evil." Later on, T. S. Eliot attacked him as an undisciplined, self-deluded heretic of "distinct sexual morbidity," and Bertrand Russell found his theory of "blood consciousness" sympathetic to Nazi ideology. An influential scholar, William York Tindall, said that "his best novel [*The Plumed Serpent*] did not make sense." Lawrence's reputation might not have recovered so vigorously from the weight of such negative views (I cite only three among the many) had it not been for more perceptive readers like Ford Madox Ford, Richard Aldington, Aldous Huxley, Catherine Carswell, and E. M. Forster ("Lawrence was the greatest imaginative novelist of his generation"), who honored and admired his work without ignoring its shortcomings.

Recent criticism has followed this direction. The leading critics of the "Lawrence revival" of the fifties, like F. R. Leavis, Harry Moore, Horace Gregory, Mark Spilka, and Mark Schorer, read Lawrence with that impelling imaginative response that Rilke likens to love. And the later generation of critics included in this book seem even more passionately involved in his work, especially those aspects previously overlooked by the earlier critics. Having absorbed the insights of their predecessors, they are perhaps less defensive about Lawrence, less concerned with justifying his place in the pantheon of great English novelists. But the real strength of these younger critics lies in their sympathy for Lawrence's radical dissent, in their understanding of his struggle

1

to create a "new consciousness" in his readers, in their appreciation of the design and of the discipline that design requires, and in their painstaking and frequently penetrating analysis of the language and structure of his fiction and poetry. They show us, in brief, fresh dimensions of Lawrence's genius.

Thus, the evidence inclines us to accept Rilke's rather challenging contention that skeptical scrutiny contributes very little of true value, while sympathetic attention often enables the reader to "grasp and hold and fairly judge" the work of the writer. Of course, this view is biased, and this book of essays is based upon that bias. It has been compiled by an editor who loves Lawrence's writing for readers who love his writing or for those who, having newly made his acquaintance, feel the pull of his power and wish to know him better. The purpose of this collection, then, is to provide the fullest sympathetic guide possible to the reading of Lawrence on either of these levels.[1]

To that end, the present selection was made with an eye on specific works and genres rather than on themes that sweep across them or on the social forces that may have influenced Lawrence's thought, though neither should be or is entirely absent. A guide of this kind, in the editor's judgment, is most useful to the reader when it serves as a companion to particular texts rather than as an index to the development of ideas, which in the case of Lawrence are not so interesting as the penumbra his sensibility casts about an individual work nor as vital as the vision that he unfolds in it. None of the essays is biographical or historical—criticism about charismatic figures such as Lawrence often mistakes the man or the myth for the work itself. Dan Jacobson's piece puts Lawrence's social and political thought in proper perspective without forgetting that Lawrence was a creative artist who must

---

[1] There are three other anthologies of Lawrence criticism worth bringing to the reader's attention: *The Achievement of D. H. Lawrence,* edited by Harry Moore and Frederick Hoffman (1953), which gives us a historical perspective of the reviews, the biographies, the memoirs, and the criticism that appeared when Lawrence was taking hold in American universities; *A D. H. Lawrence Miscellany,* edited by Harry Moore (1959), a collection of largely unpublished materials of a miscellaneous nature; and *D. H. Lawrence* (in the Twentieth Century Views series), edited by Mark Spilka (1963), a collection of scholarly articles with a valuable introduction that updates Moore's excellent history of Lawrence criticism in *Achievement.* Each of these books reflects a stage in Lawrence's reputation: signs of acceptance by the critical establishment, interest in marginalia, and reaffirmation of his status. *The D. H. Lawrence Review,* edited by James Cowan at the University of Arkansas, publishes checklists of articles from other publications, research in progress, previously unpublished letters. Laurentiana, and studies of his work. The spring 1959 issue of *Modern Fiction Studies* is devoted to Lawrence's work.

be understood through his living words and not through "historical currents."

Who better deserves the opening words about Lawrence than Lawrence himself? In "Autobiographical Sketch," written for the Curtis Brown Literary Agency while he was living near Florence, he swiftly spans his career up to *Lady Chatterley's Lover.* To complete his account, we need only a few facts that Lawrence overlooks and a summary of the last years that he recorded only in his letters.

It is important to keep in mind that Lawrence himself did not regard any part of his life as unhappy or tragic. Elsewhere, he writes:

> It is seventeen years since I gave up teaching and started to live an independent life of the pen. I have never starved, and never felt poor, though my income for the first ten years was no better, and often worse, than it would have been if I had remained an elementary school teacher. . . . I never waited in anguish for the post to bring me an answer from editor or publisher, nor did I struggle in sweat and blood to bring forth mighty works.

So *The White Peacock,* his first novel, was born without blood, sweat, and tears. It nevertheless records in faithful detail the actual physical surroundings and events of his life, and reveals, like his second novel, *The Trespasser,* a Dickensian facility for drawing unforgettable characters. However, not even his gathering powers of observation and description could hide the fact that in both novels Lawrence is clumsily trying out his craft.

Curiously enough, Lawrence makes no mention in "Autobiographical Sketch" of his two early masterpieces— *Sons and Lovers,* completed while he was residing at Lake Garda, and *Twilight in Italy,* those splendid essays of travel and place published in 1916. Along with the finest poems of *Look! We Have Come Through!,* these essays represent the fruit of his first residence in Italy, a kind of prolonged honeymoon with Frieda von Richthofen Weekley, his wife-to-be, at the Villa Igea on the shores of Garda. It was there he began writing *The Rainbow* and also *The Lost Girl,* whose last chapters are based on a brief, disastrous vacation in the wintry mountains not far from the abbey of Montecassino. Later, Lawrence was to stay briefly at the abbey on the invitation of Maurice Magnus, an American confidence man who claimed to be the son of Kaiser Wilhelm. The visit was to inspire what Lawrence himself regarded as his best piece of prose, his introduction to Magnus's *Memoirs of the Foreign Legion* (available in *Phoenix II*).

Lawrence also omits reference to *Kangaroo* (1923) and *The Boy in the Bush* (with Molly Skinner, 1924), the novels about Australia, where he spent a peaceful summer in 1922. He is also silent about *Studies in Classic American Literature* (1924), that source of so much "modern" criticism, which he had begun during the war, when he first thought of emigrating from England to America; and he makes no mention of *Psychoanalysis and the Unconscious* (1922) or *The Fantasia of the Unconscious* (1923), those remarkable books of personal philosophy (his "pollyanalytics," he used to say) conceived while he was living on the Gulf of La Spezia immediately after the war. This was a happy if not very creative period for Lawrence.

After residing in America for a time, Lawrence and Frieda returned to Italy in the fall of 1926 and let the upper floor of a *villino* near Florence (the Villa Mirenda, so called after its *padrone,* an Italian officer) where they stayed until January of 1928. In the early spring of 1927, Lawrence took a short holiday. Accompanied by an American painter, Earl Brewster, Lawrence toured the Etruscan cities of the north and afterwards wrote essays about them, which were published in magazines and posthumously collected into his third travel book about Italy, *Etruscan Places.* (The second was *Sea and Sardinia,* illustrated by Jan Juta, who now lives in Mendham, New Jersey.) That pilgrimage inspired his last important work of fiction, *The Man Who Died,* and led to another revision of *Lady Chatterley.* In July of that year, *Mornings in Mexico* appeared, a final tribute to his sojourn in the New World. Also from the New World are two short novels, *The Princess* and *St Mawr;* two short stories, "The Woman Who Rode Away" and "Blue Mocassins"; several essays on Indian rituals; and his great novel, *The Plumed Serpent.*

In January of 1928, despite failing health, he completed the third and final version of *Lady Chatterley* and supervised the arrangements for its publication at the printshop of Pino Orioli, who was to nurse him through a serious recurrence of his tubercular troubles. With the help of friends like Enid Hilton, a loyal admirer from Eastwood (his birthplace) who now lives in Ukiah, California, he distributed copies to English subscribers surreptitiously. Before long, pirated copies began to appear, and Lawrence, to protect himself, consented to a Paris paperback edition.

Meanwhile, another short-story collection *The Woman Who Rode Away,* was published in London, and the *Collected Poems,* in two volumes, made its first appearance in England three months later. However, the manuscript of his poems called *Pansies* was seized by British government officials as it came through the mail. (The poems were later printed privately by a London publisher.) Moreover, his paintings on exhibit in the Warren Gallery were confiscated as obscene in a police raid in July. In September, the Black Sun Press published his short novel *The Escaped Cock* (afterwards to be known as *The Man Who Died*).

Lawrence's health no longer permitted him to live near Florence, and most of his remaining months were spent in France, either on the Riviera or in the dry air of the mountains. In 1929, he wrote some of his finest poetry, published posthumously in Florence as *Last Poems,* and just before his death he brought out a volume of poems called *Nettles*— to sting his censors and critics. He was also able to gather together his later essays for *Assorted Articles,* though he did not live to see the book in print. He died March 2, 1930, at Vence, in the Alpes Maritimes. His remains were exhumed and carried to the Lawrence shrine at Taos, New Mexico, by Frieda and Angelo Ravagli, her third husband. Shortly after his death, an unfinished novel of 1925 appeared as *The Virgin and the Gypsy* in 1930, and the following year saw the publication of *Apocalyse,* Lawrence's final attempt to explain his beliefs rather than to embody them in a work of art. Among other posthumous publications indispensable to Lawrence readers are *Phoenix* and *Phoenix II,* the previously uncollected or unpublished prose, and the two-volume edition of the letters edited by Harry Moore. What the earlier Huxley edition suggested strongly, the Moore edition confirms: Lawrence is the finest letter writer in English since John Keats. And the *Phoenix* papers scotch the canard of those critics who maintain that Lawrence was an undisciplined, careless writer not sufficiently aware of the intellect. By themselves these letters and papers would have assured the reputation of any other writer. But not even a career as a poet and novelist of genius could make Lawrence "a little popular and rich" during his lifetime. He did not mind much nor did he seek the small success that came his way. As he says in an essay from *Assorted Articles:* "It all happened by itself and without any groans from me."

If anyone helped it to happen, it was his indefatigable wife, Frieda, who gave up children and home in order to share in the creative life of the man she loved. Though it cannot be properly called criticism, her brief reminiscence (in contrast to her garrulous *Not I, But the Wind. . .*) sums up the meaning of Lawrence's life as though time had purged her memory of all but the essence of the man. She writes:

> Though he had left his working class, he did not belong to any other, but the simplicity of a workingman's way of life was his. No servants, no luxurics, no possessions. As a very young man he had realized that they waste too much time and clutter you up. You are orderly and fresh without things, it is easy and you keep your flexibility.

How well Frieda understood the secret of his energy! No wonder he could be so productive in so relatively short a career while moving from place to place. Yet the motive of Lawrence's life, as Frieda so well knew, was to discover for himself a place where vital connections could remain intact, where a living circuit could be established between person and place. His search, with Frieda always at his side, took him from England to Italy and back to England; from England to Italy again, then Ceylon, Australia, New Mexico and Mexico and back to England; from England to America and back to Italy; from Italy to Austria and France. Each stage of the odyssey ended with the cry, "This place is no good!" Yet no one could have loved these places more than Lawrence did. In her little essay and elsewhere in her writing, Frieda bears ample testimony, as his books themselves do, to his passionate relationship with the places that entered his soul.[2]

"Lawrence's World" by Anais Nin is from her *D. H. Lawrence: An Unprofessional Study,* first published in Paris in a limited edition two years after his death. It was neglected until very recently by all but the coterie of Nin addicts, and as Harry Moore remarks in his introduction to the book, had more readers paid attention to it and less to the memoirs of the period, Lawrence's books might have been more widely read. Miss Nin contends that Lawrence had a twofold consciousness of planes of being: "the plane of the visible universe, nature, houses, churches, collieries, etc., with a plane of corresponding thought perpetually at work at its task of understanding and transforming." Then there is the plane of "subconscious life in continuous flow and movement, with its own wisdom and its own impulse." This is the subject of Miss Nin's study. It concentrates on the world of "pure passionate experience"

---

[2] For extended discussions of Lawrence's "sense of place", see Mark Schorer's introduction to *Poste Restante* (ed. Harry Moore), reprinted under the title of "Lawrence and the Spirit of Place" and Edward Nehls's, "D. H. Lawrence: The Spirit of Place" (from *The Achievement of D. H. Lawrence.*

rather than on the world of man, with particular attention to the language, themes, and symbols Lawrence employed to convey these experiences. Like Frieda's few pages, this selection from her book presents a succinct overview of the subject and opens the gates to his world.[3]

Designed as an introduction to Lawrence's third novel, Kazin's "Sons, Lovers, and Mothers" serves its purpose admirably. Kazin places the novel in its milieu: the opening pages are grounded in the conventional, matter-of-fact nineteenth-century realism exemplified by Lawrence's first two novels, but the following chapters reveal the kind of imaginative gifts we associate with early modernists like Joyce and Proust. Kazin sees *Sons and Lovers* as a novel made great by Lawrence's sense of authority, by his control over his materials, and by the shaping vision that transforms personal experience into a universal metaphor. He acknowledges the autobiographical elements, without trivializing them into simplistic Oedipal terms. Though Lawrence was acquainted with Freud's ideas before he wrote the novel, it is not, as some critics seem to think, a case history. Lawrence treats Miriam not so much a problem to be solved as a subject to be presented. In a similar manner he dramatizes Paul's struggle against the "weakness of being too much his mother's son." In contrast to the romantic sexual concept of his contemporaries, Lawrence valued love in the mythological sense of a sacred life-force connection, lacking in the relationship with Miriam, powerful in the kinship with his mother. It was this intense sympathetic bond between mother and son, broken at her death, that Lawrence ever after sought to re-create between himself and life. He succeeded in creating "exciting and fruitful" versions of it in his relationship with Frieda, his friends, and above all his work.

Since the artist has knowledge of corruption, what he creates must inevitably cope with corruption. In "The Reality of Peace"—similar statements occur in the discursive writings of 1915–19, especially in "The Crown" and the essay on Poe—Lawrence writes: "There is in me the desire of creation and the desire of dissolution. Shall I deny either? Then neither is fulfilled." From such clues, Colin Clarke develops the thesis that Lawrence had an ambivalent attitude toward corruption, that he was attracted as well as repelled by mud and machine alike (John Middleton

---

[3] Miss Nin, a women's liberationist herself, does not interpret Lawrence's attitudes toward women as those of a "male chauvinist pig," as does Kate Millett. For an amusing attack on her views, see Norman Mailer's *A Prisoner of Sex* (1971).

Murry had explored this idea in *Son of Woman*). Clarke corrects
the misimpression that Lawrence conceived of the process of reduction as necessarily negative, as a pure death-process, as an evil.
There is the Lawrence who discovered beauty in the phosphor-
escence of putrescence, who believed that we remain in deadly
isolation if we cut ourselves off from the energy of either disintegration or growth. Like Blake, Lawrence was open to all forms of
essential life-force and refused to be bound even by his own terms.
Lawrence's attitude toward "will" or the machine-principle, toward sensational or disintegrative sex is much more equivocal than
is usually conceded. In *The Rainbow,* wholeness is to be achieved,
paradoxically, by at once resisting and incorporating the mechanical and the corrupt. This duality of view, translated into characterization, produced a curious kind of "split" personality in
Skrebensky and Ursula.

David Cavitch's analysis of the sequel, *Women in Love* (Mark
Schorer rates this discussion as "the very best we have had on that
extremely difficult novel") links the aesthetic symbolism with
what he regards as a pervasive sexual ambivalency. Cavitch contends that the theme of sexual ambivalence reveals unresolved
conflicts in Lawrence's own psyche (whereas Colin Clarke prefers
to take it as a form of resolution, in the same sense that Dos-
toyevsky insisted on the necessity of ambivalence as a final
attitude). Birkin, as the reader may find, is intended to be a man
who expresses sexual affection and unconscious feelings in every
relationship with things and persons—not merely the opposite sex.
Yet Birkin more powerfully craves a homoerotic relationship with
Gerald—the discarded "Prologue" to the novel is cited as evidence
of this dominant drive. But Gerald, whom Cavitch regards as the
central erotic presence of the novel, cannot bring himself to accept
the relationship, backs off, and continues his "process of dissolution" in his affair with Gudrun. The ideal of manly love ends in
catastrophe, and Lawrence's heartbreak over the suicide of Gerald
is unmatched in his work except at the conclusion of *Sons and
Lovers,* where Lawrence suffers with Paul over the death of his
mother (says Cavitch). Thus, love fails to be fully theraputic, and
that failure results from the fracturing of the homoerotic ideal.
Birkin is left incomplete, the future of his relationship to Ursula
uncertain, and Lawrence's attitude toward women seems more
acutely ambivalent than before. One may disagree with Cavitch,
but not without admitting that he presents the complex realities
of the novel in fresh focus.

To a generation of readers rebelling against all stifling forms
of human relationship as a denial of Self, *Aaron's Rod* makes more

sense than it did to most contemporaries of Lawrence (he wrote Donald Carswell from Fontana Vecchia in Taormina in 1921 that everyone, even Frieda, hated the book, except Thomas Seltzer, his American publisher). Misunderstood and underestimated even by such otherwise sound critics as Julian Moynahan, Eliseo Vivas, H. M. Daleski, and David Daiches, it has long required the extended sympathetic reexamination that Yudhishtar gives it in "The Changing Scene," an excerpt from his *Conflict in the Novels of D. H. Lawrence.* Rather than a break or decline in Lawrence's development as a novelist, *Aaron's Rod* represents to Yudhishtar a continuation of his "life and thought" adventure where *Women in Love* had left it. Lawrence explores the theme of man-woman relationship, bringing out its limitations and inadequacies, but he has shifted his interest to something else—an attempt to define man's need for coming into possession of his own soul, of freeing women as well as men for "isolate self-responsibility." The novel contains the most forceful statement of Lawrence's view that a person's first responsibility is to himself, to his own soul within him, an elaboration of a statement made to a friend: "Love isn't all that important: one's own free soul is first." Yudhishtar shows how this quest for a free, proud, single Being-hood unites many of the seemingly unrelated episodes and makes intelligible Aaron's flight from his family. Kate Millett's description of the novel as "strident and unpleasant" (*Sexual Politics,* 1970) seems narrowminded.

Anthony Beal, in the selection from his *D. H. Lawrence,* goes along with most criticism of *Kangaroo* insofar as he feels that Lawrence's compulsive need to retell the nightmare experiences of wartime England severely disrupts the story at a crucial point, allowing the violent emotions of those years to spill over onto the Australian scene. Despite this weakness in the structure, Beal recognizes the attractions of the novel: the "spirit of place" is evoked most brilliantly, and there is a coherent progression of thought and belief. When Somers rejects Kangaroo's offer of a homoerotic relationship, it may be assumed that Lawrence is no longer concerned with the idea of conjunction between two men. Signs of a new interest begin to appear, hinted at in "The Crown" and chapters 3 and 5 of *Fantasia of the Unconscious:* "no longer women, no longer men, no longer political power . . . but the gods." At first it seems possible that they may manifest themselves in the figure of Kangaroo, but Kangaroo becomes cast as the alter ego to Somers/Lawrence, and the dark gods remain hidden, waiting to be summoned from the fierce primitive earth of Mexico.

In "The Lost Trail," Keith Sagar analyzes the structure and

texture of *The Plumed Serpent,* with close attention to key passages. Drawing on Lawrence's other works of the same period for confirmation or elucidation, he uncovers the novel's inner coherence and judges its achievement against its own apparent intention[4] rather than against formal preconceptions, which have vitiated so much Lawrence criticism. Sagar sees Don Ramon, not Kate Leslie, as the center of Lawrence's magnificent construct, For Don Ramon, the return of Quetzalcoatl is the return of the great god Pan, the "quick of all beings and existence." His self-appointed task is to transform the fanged serpent of the animistic Aztecs into a new version of the godhead within all living things. He is to create, as it were, a phoenix. Kate Leslie, drifting toward nullity, is initiated into the mysteries of this power by Cipriano, and she wins her soul out of the chaos. Her marriage to him offers passivity and abandon, but at the price of surrendering everything else, including her newly won sense of selfhood. She cannot submit wholly to the "great pliant column" of Cipriano nor to the "older consciousness" she occasionally experiences with him and with Don Ramon. Mexico has no final answers for her. At the end, revitalized, she leaves the pursuit of dark gods to Mexicans and prepares to seek elsewhere for the clue to human relationship (unlike Lou Witt, in *St. Mawr,* who cancels the quest).

In *The Dark Sun,* perhaps the first study of Lawrence that took into serious account all aspects of his work, Graham Hough writes with amenity and quiet humor, and can be deft enough to make his point about *Lady Chatterley's Lover* by an apt quotation from Doctor Johnson. In his more discursive passages, he taps the resources of a mature normality which in the excerpt included here makes a sympathetic contact with Lawrence's intense and sometimes agitated insights.

Hough traces the basic shift of interest from the lyrical outer fabric of life to the radical inner forces of personality or cultural changes. This shift is accompanied by a movement toward emancipation, which is also a bewilderment and geographic uprooting. In *Lady Chatterley,* Lawrence has circled back toward his home place and the original sources of his power. His depiction of Tavershall and his Dickensian portrait of Mrs. Bolton show him writing with unequaled confidence and craft, and his introduction to

---

[4] L. D. Clark's "Metal to Membrane" in *Dark Night of the Body* is the most meticulous and extensive study of *The Plumed Serpent* that I have read, but it is too long to include in this book. Jascha Kessler's "Descent in Darkness' in Moore's *D. H. Lawrence Miscellany* is an excellent and intelligent study of the mythic elements of the novel.

Connie's English background and situation is one of Lawrence's most accomplished pieces of straightforward narrative. There is the intimate, closely observed relationship between two people otherwise separated by class and condition, which created an issue Lawrence decided not to evade—how to say candidly what love making is. The "phallic consciousness" (described in detail for the first time, except in pornography) evolves into a sensual tenderness, a resolution of the opposing forces represented by Miriam and Clara in *Sons and Lovers*. That personal tenderness is placed against the impersonal spectre of industrialized England and against the machine mentality. Lawrence did not hold, as his detractors have alleged, that England could be saved by sex alone, but he did believe that a living sense of human reality rooted in sensual tenderness and fidelity could preserve the plane of consciousness that Anäis Nin describes in "Lawrence's World."

Monroe Engel values Lawrence's short fiction as a genre distinct from his novels rather than an extension of them, as critics have often assumed it to be. He discerns certain nuclear symbols, themes, and patterns, and devices for vivifying them, that link the short novels in an inevitable progression. These links are (1) at the outset, a disordered relationship against which the protagonist must choose between an old, conventional love characterized by sanity and a sense of over-responsibility and a new kind of relationship the nature of which is suggested with increasing exactness and coherence as Lawrence's art develops; (2) an objective style that becomes increasingly visionary and magical, from *The Fox* to *The Man Who Died;* (3) a finale that is almost always visionary, rhetorical, and abstract until Lawrence's mature art permitted him to dramatize it in events; and (4) animal imagery that reinforces the meaning of the novel and gives it "feeling tone." Lawrence's growth as an artist, Engel maintains, can be traced through his short novels alone; indeed, Engel finds that Lawrence must be judged as the most successful practicioner of that form in English literature. Engel discourages the condescending view that Lawrence turned to his briefer fictions as a kind of vacation from his more ambitious projects, or that he reworked refractory material from them into unquestionably minor narratives.[5]

[5] In his short study called *D. H. Lawrence,* Anthony West has an outstanding chapter on Lawrence's tales, containing the most careful analysis of the texture of his prose up to that time (1951), but West's flippant and offhand deprecation of the work is intolerable. Also there are errors of fact (e.g., in the discussion of "The Woman Who Rode Away"). Yet the book is useful because West remembers meetings between H. G. Wells and Lawrence. Leavis, Hough, and Moynahan also have excellent chapters on the tales, but they are too extensive for inclusion here.

The reader immersed in Lawrence the fictionalist may find it strange that Lawrence once thought of himself primarily as a poet. Not until his complete poetry became available once more in two volumes (edited in 1964 by Vivian de Sola Pinto and Warren Roberts) did most critics realize how extensively, variously, and magnificently Lawrence had expressed himself in verse. Writers like Kenneth Rexroth proved to be prophetic. Five years earlier, Rexroth performed an invaluable service by bringing forth a cross section of Lawrence's poetry in an inexpensive paperback, brilliantly introduced with a poet's discrimination. No doubt the success of this little volume and the probity of his praise had some influence on the decision to republish all of Lawrence's poetry. Rexroth holds that the early Lawrence, despite his emotional hunger and frustration, was the best of the Georgian poets; and after awakening from the sleep that followed his mother's death, the best of the imagist poets; and having developed an accuracy of observation that must haunt the memory, wrote some of the finest free verse in the language. And in the epigrams and political poems, often dismissed as disheveled drafts, Rexroth finds the "noble disorder" of great poetry. And the mystery of *The Plumed Serpent* is distilled into those "intense, direct, passionate" hymns to the dark gods, which Rexroth believes contain also Lawrence's personal religion. In his last poems, Rexroth sees a transcendant tranquility of spirit, a state of grace and acceptance before his final journey. Examined in their poetic, personal,[5] and cultural contexts, the poems are a long continuous paean to life lived fully in the flesh and in the spirit, and R. P. Blackmur's attack on Lawrence as a poet without a mask (if not a typical judgment, one too often accepted) seems to confirm at least the first part of Rilke's contention.

Dan Jacobson, himself a novelist, believes that Lawrence's tremendous power as an artist was generated by his "intense and unremitting" hatred of modern society. Between *The Rainbow* and *The Plumed Serpent,* Lawrence worked out a doctrine of human nature and society, argues Jacobson, that we will find argued most successfully from novel to novel rather than in his discursive books and essays. Lawrence's doctrine— that the catastrophic uprooting of man from nature began with the Industrial Revolution— belongs

---

[6] One of Rexroth's speculations is in error ("probably the girl's name was not Helen")—the Helen of the early poems was Helen Corke, a teacher from the Croydon days with whom Lawrence had an affair. Joyce Carol Oates's review of *The Complete Poems* in *The American Poetry Review* Nov./Dec. 1972 is the best short appreciation I know.

to the tradition of protest against nineteenth-century industrialism, but it goes beyond mere protest in its passionate plea for balance, in its quest for corrective polarity, in its profound sense of the interdependence of all forms of life. In retrospect, this doctrine, Jacobson declares, is revolutionary and radical next to the proposals of other reformers, modern or otherwise, and Lawrence's hatred of society proved to be healthy for his art. Jacobson's views are certainly disputable (compare them, for instance, with Colin Clarke's), but if nothing else they do expose the imbecility of Sir Charles Snow's remark that Lawrence was guilty of "imbecilic and anti-social feelings," when indeed Lawrence foresaw the perils of our present age. An exception to Rilke's belief that art cannot be "reached . . . with criticism," this essay takes Lawrence out of the hands of humanitarians, women's liberationists, and other idealists who ignore his intense "feeling for the individuality of consciousness" and his fierce commitment to a sense of community with the world.

Had space permitted, I would have included an essay on Lawrence's criticism (which despite its occasionally crotchiness was usually very penetrating), one on his "pollyanalytics," and one on his travel books. It was especially in the latter that Lawrence caught the unique flavor, captured the especial spirit of his surroundings, no matter how brief the visit (as his tour of Sardinia and his pilgrimage to the Etruscan cities) or how extended the stay (as his residence at Lake Garda and in Mexico). The polarities of his fiction and poetry are reflected in the polarities he discovered in the visible world: the natural unspoiled place corrupted by unnatural circumstances and the march of civilization, the difference between flowers growing in a sunny field and men working in a coal mine. But there should be enough in this volume to indicate that Lawrence's genius knew almost no boundaries.

D. H. Lawrence

Autobiographical Sketch

David Herbert Lawrence—born 11 Sept. 1885 in Eastwood, Nottingham, a small mining town in the Midlands—father a coal-miner, scarcely able to read or write—Mother from the bour-geoisie, the cultural element in the house (let them [*struck out*] read *Sons & Lovers,* the first part is all autobiography—you might send them a copy [*struck out*]).—Fourth of five children—two brothers oldest—then a sister, then D. H.— then another sister— always delicate health but strong constitution—went to elemen-tary school & was just like anybody else of the miners' children—at age of twelve won a scholarship for Nottingham High School, considered best day school in England—purely bourgeois school— quite happy there, but the scholarship boys were a class apart— D. H. made a couple of bourgeois friendships, but they were odd fish,—he instinctively recoiled away from the bourgeoisie, regular sort—left school at 16—had a severe illness—made the acquaint-ance of Miriam and her family, who lived on a farm, and who really roused him to critical & creative consciousness (see *Sons & Lovers*). Taught in a rough & fierce elementary school of mining boys: salary, first year, £ 5.—second year £ 10—third year £ 15— (from age of 17 to 21)—Next two years in Nottingham University, at first quite happy, then utterly bored.—Again the same feeling of boredom with the middle-classes, & recoil away from them in-stead of moving towards them & rising in the world. Took B.A. course, but dropped it; used to write bits of poems & patches of *The White Peacock* during lectures. These he wrote for Miriam, the girl on the farm, who was herself becoming a school-teacher. She thought it all wonderful—else, probably, he would never have written—His own family strictly "natural" looked on such performance as writing as "affectation." Therefore wrote in secret at home. Mother came upon a chapter of *White Peacock*—read it quizzically, & was amused. "But my boy, how do you know it was like that? You don't know—" She thought one ought to know—

Autobiographical Sketch *by D. H. Lawrence. Reprinted by permission of Lawrence Pollinger Ltd., the estate of the late Mrs. Frieda Lawrence, and the Viking Press, Inc.*

and she hoped her son, who was "clever," might one day be a professor or a clergyman or perhaps even a little Mr. Gladstone. That would have been rising in the world—on the ladder. Flights of genius were nonsense—you had to be clever & rise in the world, step by step.—D. H. however recoiled away from the world, hated its ladder, & refused to rise. He had proper bourgeois aunts with "library" & "drawing-room" to their houses—but didn't like that either—preferred the powerful life in a miner's kitchen—& still more, the clatter of nailed boots in the little kitchen of Miriam's farm. Miriam was even poorer than he—but she loved poetry and consciousness and flight of fancy above all. So he wrote for her— still without any idea of becoming a literary man at all—looked on himself as just a school-teacher—& mostly hated school-teaching. Wrote *The White Peacock* in bits and snatches, between age of 19 and 24. Most of it written six or seven times.

At the age of twenty-three, left Nottingham college & went for the first time to London, to be a teacher in a boys' school in Croydon, £ 90. a year. Already the intense physical dissatisfaction with Miriam. Miriam read all his writings—she alone. His mother, whom he loved best on earth, he never spoke to, about his writing. It would have been a kind of "showing-off," or affectation. It was Miriam who sent his poems to Ford Madox Hueffer, who had just taken over *The English Review*. This was when D. H. was 24. Hueffer accepted, wrote to Lawrence, and was most kind and most friendly. Got Heinemann to accept the MS., a ragged & bulky mass, of *The White Peacock*—invited the school-teacher to lunch—introduce him to Edward Garnett—and Garnett became a generous and genuine friend. Hueffer & Garnett launched D. H. into the literary world. Garnett got Duckworth to accept the first book of poems: *Love Poems and Others*. When Lawrence was 25, *The White Peacock* appeared. But before the day of publication, his mother died—she just looked once at the advance copy, held it in her hand—

The death of his mother wiped out everything else—books published, or stories in magazines. It was the great crash, and the end of his youth. He went back to Croydon to the hated teaching— the £ 50 for *The White Peacock* paid the doctor etc for his mother.

Then a weary and bitter year—broke with Miriam—and again fell dangerously ill with pneumonia. Got slowly better. Was making a little money with stories, Austin Harrison, who had taken over *The English Review,* being a staunch supporter, and Garnett and Hueffer staunch backers. In May, 1912, went away suddenly with his present wife, of German birth, daughter of Baron Friedrich von Richthofen. They went to Metz, then Bavaria, then-Italy—and the new phase had begun. He was 26—his youth was over—there came a great gap between him and it.

Was in Italy and Germany the greater part of the time between 1912 & 1914. In England during the period of the war—pretty well isolated. In 1915 *The Rainbow* was suppressed for immorality—and the sense of detachment from the bourgeois world, the world which controls press, publication and all, became almost complete. He had no interest in it, no desire to be at one with it. Anyhow the suppression of *The Rainbow* had proved it impossible. Henceforth he put away any idea of "success," of succeeding with the British bourgeois public, and stayed apart.

Left England in 1919, for Italy—had a house for two years in Taormina, Sicily. In 1920 was published in America *Women in Love*—which every publisher for four years had refused to accept, because of *The Rainbow* scandal. In Taormina wrote *The Lost Girl, Sea and Sardinia,* and most of *Aaron's Rod.* In 1922 sailed from Naples to Ceylon, and lived in Kandy for a while—then on to Australia for a time—in each case taking a house and settling down. Then sailed from Sydney to San Francisco, and went to Taos, in New Mexico, where he settled down again with his wife, near the Pueblo of the Indians. Next year he acquired a small ranch high up on the Rocky Mountains, looking west to Arizona. Here, and in Old Mexico, where he travelled and lived for about a year, he stayed till 1926, writing *St. Mawr* in New Mexico, and the final version of *The Plumed Serpent* down in Oaxaca in Old Mexico.

Came to England 1926—but cannot stand the climate. For the last two years has lived in a villa near Florence, where *Lady Chatterley's Lover* was written.*

---

*A biographical appendix to this autobiographical account will be found in the editor's introduction. [*ed. note.*]

Frieda Lawrence

D. H. Lawrence, the Failure

From time to time another man sits down and writes a book or article with great gusto that D. H. Lawrence was a failure. As he sits at his desk that perhaps overlooks a campus, securely and comfortably he says to himself, "I thank my stars that I am not like that man Lawrence."

But as we are human beings, not elephants or snowbirds or submarines, it is our business to come off as much as we can as human beings and as such Lawrence was not a failure. When Mr. Ford* somewhere says: "I would not give five cents for all the art in the world," it is funny, but there is a spot of failure there. Hitler may be a great mechanizer, but as a human being he seems a failure.

A child is born into the world in a special setting and most likely remains inside this setting all his life. He can't get out. That is particularly true of Europe. In America it is not so much so. A child takes this setting into its consciousness and adjusts itself to it or maybe questions it. Now the slice of time between birth and death is not so very long and the opportunities for the weaving of our life are limited. There are not so many strands to weave with.

First there is the mother and the family. Lawrence gave himself with all his loving power to his mother. He wanted to fill up the empty, sad space that life had left in her; a task too heavy for any child, it left him with a fear of women. He was born into the working class. He knew the working class with a basic knowledge, their immediate response to all that went on around them, their warmhearted generosity and their incapacity to abstract and to really think. This last was his tragedy, that they could not think or follow him; primarily he wrote for them, because he loved them.

*This is the Ford Madox Hueffer Lawrence speaks about in his autobiographical sketch. Hueffer changed his name to Ford. [ed. note]

From The Memoirs and Correspondence by Frieda Lawrence, edited by E. W. Tedlock, Jr. William Heinemann Ltd., 1961. Copyright © 1961, 1961 by the Estate of Frieda Lawrence. Reprinted by permission of Lawrence Pollinger Ltd., the estate of the late Mrs. Frieda Lawrence, and Alfred A. Knopf, Inc.

This capacity for love but not blind love, but a very seeing one
was the essence of him. Also the absolute need to investigate all
his relationships to their very roots. He took the responsibility of
all he did very thoroughly, he thought and pondered and then
came to his conclusion and stuck to it.

From his mother he got the almost puritan sense of responsibility and from his father the fun of the immediate living, quick
and often violent in reaction. But besides the responsibility of his
own life, he felt it was up to him to give a direction to the way
humanity was going, to help make the cat jump the right way.
He himself and the people he met and all he saw and sensed were
the sounding board. It was personal or impersonal at the same
time. He did not lay down any God Almighty rules and laws for his
fellowmen but said to them as it were: here are in my books my
honest-to-God experiences and my conclusions, take it or leave
it, you will most likely leave it.

He had an uncanny sense of what was real and what was not.
And as we all cling to our unrealities like leeches he had terrific
fights with all his friends. He could not let anything phoney pass.
So he was much on the warpath. Long before Hitler he had said
that it is not the intellect but the blood that makes the wheels go
round. But he wanted the blood of all races to function purely.
And his final conclusion was that only human relations, good
human relations, can save the world. Here lies the final sanity.

No man got so much out of living as Lawrence did. Nothing
was dull from morning to night and all along. Though he had left
his working class, he did not belong to any other, but the simplicity
of a workingman's way of life was his. No servants, no luxuries,
no possessions. As a very young man he had realized that they
waste too much time and clutter you up. You are orderly and fresh
without things, it is easy and you keep your flexibility. In the machine Lawrence saw a deadly enemy of man, man was no longer
the God in the machine but the machine had become God. Then
he traveled. I doubt whether he ever thought he would find a
ready-made Utopia anywhere. He loved just going to look at the
world. He knew too well that a man makes his own heaven and
hell. But he looked at the different places he visited with infinite
gusto, getting their essence as it were through his skin. There was
gusto even in his disgust. He knew how rotten Europe was, nobody
better, and he hated it, but never lost his deep belief in a renewal
of its oldness; he was a stepping stone from the old to the new;
he chose the Phoenix for his symbol. How he loved work, work of

every kind, the serious job of writing, the fun of putting a nail in, or making a chair or a mat, anything. He lived in the extreme sense of the word every moment of his forty-four years, the whole of him lived, flesh and bones and thoughts.

Does this sound like a failure? And then death looked him in the face. He looked back at him and did not flinch, though it was hard. Because it is up to a man to die decently. So he faced the oncoming death like another adventure, something else he had to tackle. He tackled it to the end.

If Lawrence's life was a failure then I long for more failures like his in our day.

Anäis Nin

Lawrence's World

In the beginning, the idyllic beginning, when difficulties are felt only through a half-dim consciousness, Lawrence has ample freedom to observe the background, and we have the classical, almost naïve surface landscape painting of the *White Peacock*.

As Lawrence the poet evolves, the background becomes ominous, as in *Sons and Lovers*. Further on it becomes symbolical, as in *Twilight in Italy*. There, while descriptions of nature are richer than ever, it is their reflection in the mind and feelings which becomes more essential. As he discovers the universe and pierces the crust of the earth with his personal vision, the background becomes more and more symbolical.

And now begins in Lawrence that consciousness of planes: of twofold and multiple planes.

There is the plane of the visible universe, nature, houses, churches, collieries, movies—the artist's eye sees them all; there is the plane of corresponding thought perpetually at work at its task of understanding and transforming. This is all an upper plane, in the head, the brain. Then there is the plane of subconscious life in continuous flow and movement, with its own wisdom and its own impulses: the solar plexus, the blood-consciousness. (Blake's *Marriage of Heaven and Hell*.) "The blood consciousness is the first and last knowledge of the living soul: the depths."

". . . The absolute need which one has for some sort of satisfactory mental attitude toward oneself and things in general makes one try to abstract some definite conclusions from one's experiences as a writer and as a man. The novels and poems are *pure passionate experiences*. These" (the two books on Psychology) "are made afterwards, from the experiences."

So we shall first study the experiences.

Since his world is the enlargement of his own gigantic imagination, out to see and to experience all, the characters have their roots in reality, but they are soon dissociated from familiar molds and absorbed by Lawrence. He is at work on such a vast, almost impersonal comprehension, that realities are not sufficient: he must use symbols.

Probabilities of the literal kind do not bother him, and his dialogue is as often impossible as possible, his situations unreal as real. He is outside of that. A great part of his writing might be called "interlinear" because of his constant effort to make conscious and articulate the silent subconscious communications between human beings.

First of all he asks us to begin at the beginning of the world with him. By his own questions, put as seriously as a child's, and with a child's obstinacy, he will take each man back to the beginning of the world, as if each had to settle it all for himself, begin his own world, find his god. *(The Boy in the Bush.)*

To retrogress with Lawrence is to question every value, and thus begins his reversal of ordinary values.

It is an effort to recapture genuine evaluations, like those of children before they are taught. A child will say to an older person who has been playing with him and participating whole-heartedly in his make-believe: Are you older than me? How can that be?

How can that be if the older person has been playing, conceiving fancies with him? The child does not see any difference, if age is a closeness to death, and death is simply not being able to play, not being alive in feeling. The child is looking *at the essence quality of livingness,* not at any outward appearance of age, which is irrelevant.

Thus Lawrence says with the same pure, profound disregard of appearances: everything is either alive or dead, according to transcendental definitions of life and death.

Lawrence's chief preoccupation is precisely the choice between life and death, or rather: between *complete life and death. Livingness* is the axis of his world, the light, the gravitation, and electromagnetism of his world.

Alfred Kazin

Sons, Lovers, and Mothers

[In the years since *Sons and Lovers* was first published (1913),] how many autobiographical novels have been written by young men about the mothers they loved too well, about their difficulties in "adjusting" to other women, and about themselves as the sensitive writers-to-be who liberated themselves just in time in order to write their first novel? Such autobiographical novels—psychological devices they usually are, written in order to demonstrate freedom from the all-too-beloved mother—are one of the great symbols of our time. They are rooted in the modern emancipation of women. Lawrence himself, after a return visit in the 1920's to his native Nottinghamshire, lamented that the "wildness" of his father's generation was gone, that the dutiful sons in his own generation now made "good" husbands. Even working-class mothers in England, in the last of the Victorian age, had aimed at a "higher" standard of culture, and despising their husbands and concentrating on their sons, they had made these sons images of themselves. These mothers had sought a new dignity and even a potential freedom for themselves as women, but holding their sons too close, they robbed them of their necessary "wildness" and masculine force. So the sons grew up in bondage to their mothers, and the more ambitious culturally these sons were—Frank O'Connor says that *Sons and Lovers* is the work of "one of the New Men who are largely a creation of the Education Act of 1870"—the more likely they were to try for their emancipation by writing a novel. The cultural aspiration that explains their plight was expected to turn them into novelists.

Sons and Lovers (which is not a first novel) seems easy to imitate. One reason, apart from the relationships involved, is the very directness and surface conventionality of its technique. James Joyce's *A Portrait of the Artist As a Young Man,* published only three years after *Sons and Lovers,* takes us immediately into the "new" novel of the twentieth century. It opens on a bewildering series of images faithful to the unconsciousness of childhood. Proust, who brought out the first volume of his great novel, *A la*

From the "Introduction" to the Modern Library edition of Sons and Lovers. *Reprinted by permission of the author*

recherche du temps perdu, in the same year that Lawrence published *Sons and Lovers,* imposed so highly stylized a unity of mood on the "Ouverture" to *Du coté de chez Swann,* that these impressions of childhood read as if they had been reconstructed to make a dream. But *Sons and Lovers* opens a a nineteenth-century novel with a matter-of-fact description of the setting—the mine, the landscape of "Bestwood," the neighboring streets and houses. This opening could have been written by Arnold Bennett, or any other of the excellent "realists" of the period whose work does not summon up, fifty years later, the ecstasy of imagination that Lawrence's work, along with that of Joyce and Proust, does provide to us. Lawrence is writing close to the actual facts. In his old-fashioned way he is even writing *about* the actual facts. No wonder that a young novelist with nothing but *his* own experiences to start him off may feel that Lawrence's example represents the triumph of experience. Literature has no rites in *Sons and Lovers;* everything follows as if from memory alone. When the struggle begins that makes the novel—the universal modern story of a "refined" and discontented woman who pours out on her sons the love she refuses the husband too "common" for her—the equally universal young novelist to whom all this has happened, the novelist who in our times is likely to have been all too mothered and fatherless, cannot help saying to himself—"Why can't I write this good a novel out of myself? Haven't I suffered as much as D. H. Lawrence and am I not just as sensitive? And isn't this a highly selective age in which 'sensitive' writers count?"

But the most striking thing about Lawrence—as it is about Paul Morel in *Sons and Lovers*—is his sense of his own authority. Though he was certainly not saved from atrocious suffering in relation to his mother, Lawrence's "sensitivity" was in the main concerned with reaching the highest and widest possible consciousness of everything—"nature," family, society, books—that came within his experience as a human being. His sense of his own powers, of himself as a "medium" through which the real life in things could be discovered for other people, was so strong that his personal vividness stayed with his earliest friends as a reminder of the best hopes of their youth; it was instantly recognized by literary people in London when they read his work. You can easily dislike Lawrence for this air of authority, just as many people dislike him for the influence that he exerted during his lifetime and that has grown steadily since his death in 1930. There is already an unmistakeable priggish conceit about Paul Morel in this novel. Here is a miner's son who is asked by his mother if his is a "divine discontent" and replies in this style: "Yes, I don't care about its divinity. But damn your happiness! So long as life's full, it doesn't matter whether it's happy or not. I'm afraid your happiness would bore me." But even this contains Lawrence's sense of his own authority. He saw his talent as a sacred possession—he was almost too proud to think of his career as a *literary* one. This sense of having a power that makes for righteousness—this was so strong in Lawrence, and so intimately associated with his mother's influence, that the struggle he describes in *Sons and Lovers,* the struggle to love another woman as he had loved his mother, must be seen as the connection he made between his magic "demon," his gift, and his relationship to his mother.

Freud once wrote that he who is a favorite of the mother becomes a "conqueror." This was certainly Freud's own feeling about himself. The discoverer of the Oedipus complex never doubted that the attachment which, abnormally protracted, makes a son feel that loving any woman but his mother is a "desecration," nevertheless, in its early prime features, gives a particular kind of strength to the son. It is a spiritual strength, not the masculine "wildness" that Lawrence was to miss in contemporary life. Lawrence's own feeling that he was certainly somebody, the pride that was to sustain him despite horribly damaged lungs through so many years of tuberculosis until his death at forty-five; the pride that carried him so far from a miner's cottage; the pride that enabled him, a penniless school-teacher, to run off with a German baroness married to his old teacher and to make her give up her three children; the pride that thirty years after his death still makes him so vivid to us as we read—this pride had not its origin but its *setting,* in the fierce love of Mrs. Arthur Lawrence for "Bert," of Mrs. Morel for her Paul.

Lawrence, who was so full of his own gift, so fully engaged in working it out that he would not acknowledge his gifted contemporaries, certainly did feel that the "essential soul" of him as he would have said, his special demon, his particular gift of vision, his particular claim on immortality, was bound up with his mother. Not "love" in the psychological sense of conscious consideration, but love in the mythological sense of a sacred connection, was what Lawrence associated with his mother and Paul with Mrs. Morel. Lawrence's power over others is directly traceable to his own sense of the sacredness still possible to life, arising from the powers hidden in ordinary human relationships. The influence he had—if only temporarily—even on a rationalist like Bertrand Russell reminds one of the hold he kept on socialist working-class people he had grown up with and who certainly did not share Lawrence's exalted individualism. Lawrence's "authority," which made him seem unbearably full of himself to those who disliked him, was certainly of a very singular kind. He had an implicit confidence in his views on many questions—on politics as on sex and love; he was able to pontificate in later life about the Etruscans, of whom he knew nothing, as well as to talk dangerous nonsense about "knowing through the blood" and the leader principle. Yet it is Lawrence's struggle to retain all the moral authority that he identified with his mother's love that explains the intensity of *Sons and Lovers,* as it does the particular intensity of Lawrence's style in this book, which he later criticized as too violent. Yet behind this style lies Lawrence's lifelong belief in what he called "quickness," his need to see the "shimmer," the life force in everything, as opposed to the "dead crust" of its external form. Destiny for Lawrence meant his privileged and constant sense of the holiness implicit in this recognition of the life force. Destiny also meant his recognition, as a delicate boy who had already seen his older brother Ernest (the "William" of *Sons and Lovers*) sicken and die of the struggle to attach himself to another woman, that his survival was somehow bound up with fidelity to his mother, Lawrence had absolute faith in his gift, but it was bound up with his physical existence which was always on trial. He felt that it was in his mother's hands. The gift of life, so particularly precious to him after his near-fatal pneumonia at seventeen (when his brother died), could be easily lost.

With so much at stake, Lawrence put into ultimate terms, life or death, the struggle between Paul Morel's need to hold onto his mother and his desire to love Miriam Leivers as well. The struggle in *Sons and Lovers* is not between love of the mother and love of a young woman; it is the hero's struggle to *keep* the mother as his special strength, never to lose her, not to offend or even to vex her by showing too much partiality to other women. This is why the original of "Miriam Leivers," Jessie Chambers, says in her touching memoir (*D. H. Lawrence: A Personal Record,* by "E.T.") that she had to break with Lawrence after she had seen the final draft of the book, that "the shock of *Sons and Lovers* gave the death-blow to our friendship," for in that book "Lawrence handed his mother the laurels of victory."

That is indeed what Lawrence did; it would not have occurred to him to do anything else. And Jessie Chambers also honestly felt that she minded this for Lawrence's sake, not her own, since by this time there was no longer any question of marriage between them. Jessie, who certainly loved Lawrence for his genius even after she had relinquished all personal claim on him, had launched Lawrence's career by sending out his poems. When Lawrence, after his mother's death, wrote a first draft of *Sons and Lovers,* he was still unable to work out his situation in a novel. Jessie encouraged him to drop this unsatisfactory version of the later novel and to portray the emotional struggle directly. At his request, she even wrote out narrative sections which Lawrence revised and incorporated into his novel. (Lawrence often had women write out passages for his novels when he wanted to know how a woman would react to a particular situation; Frieda Lawrence was to contribute to his characterization of Mrs. Morel.) Lawrence sent Jessie parts of the manuscript for her comments and further notes. After so much help and even collaboration, Jessie felt betrayed by the book. Lawrence had failed to show, she said, how important a role the girl had played in the development of the young man as an artist. "It was his old inability to face his problem squarely. His mother had to be supreme, and for the sake of that supremacy every disloyalty was permissible."

Lawrence is quoted in Harry T. Moore's biography, *The Intelligent Heart,* as saying of Miriam-Jessie, she "encouraged my demon. But alas, it was me, not he, whom she loved. So for her too it was a catastrophe. My demon is not easily loved: whereas the ordinary me is. So poor Miriam was let down." Lawrence's tone is exalted, but he certainly justified himself in *Sons and Lovers* as a novelist, not as a "son." That is the only consideration now. Jessie Chambers herself became an embittered woman. She tried to find her salvation in politics, where the fierce hopes of her generation before 1914 for a new England were certainly not fulfilled. But Lawrence, taking the new draft of *Sons and Lovers* with him to finish in Germany after he had run off with Frieda, was able, if not to "liberate" himself from his mother in his novel, to write a great novel out of his earliest life and struggles.

That is the triumph Jessie Chambers would not acknowledge in *Sons and Lovers,* this she could not see—the Lawrence "unable to face his problem squarely" made a great novel out of the "problem," out of his mother, father, brother, the miners, the village, the youthful sweetheart. Whatever Jessie may have thought from being too close to Lawrence himself, whatever Lawrence may have said about his personal struggles during the six-week frenzy in which he launched the new draft, Lawrence felt his "problem" not as something to be solved, but as a subject to be represented. All these early experiences weighed on him with a pressure that he was able to communicate—later he called it "that hard violent style full of sensation and presentation." Jessie Chambers herself described Lawrence's accomplishment when she said, speaking of the new draft of *Sons and Lovers* that she drove Lawrence to write, "It was his power to transmute the common experiences into significance that I always felt to be Lawrence's greatest gift. He did not distinguish between small and great happenings. The common round was full of mystery, awaiting interpretation. Born and bred of working people, he had the rare gift of seeing them from within, and revealing them on their own plane."

Lawrence's particular gift was this ability to represent as valuable anything that came his way. He had the essential religious attribute of *valuing* life, of seeing the most trivial things as a kind of consecration. In part, at least, one can trace this to the poverty, austerity and simplicity of his upbringing. Jessie Chambers once watched Lawrence and his father gathering watercress for tea. "Words cannot convey Lawrence's brimming delight in all these simple things." Delight in simple things is one of the recurring features of the working-class existence described in *Sons and Lovers*. We can understand better the special value that Lawrence identified with his mother's laboriousness and self-denial in the scene where Mrs. Morel, wickedly extravagant, comes home clutching the pot that cost her fivepence and the bunch of pansies and daisies that cost her fourpence. The rapture of the commonest enjoyments and simplest possessions is represented in the mother and father as well as in the young artist Paul, the future D. H. Lawrence. This autobiographical novel rooted in the writer's early struggles is charged with feeling for his class, his region, his people. Lawrence was not a workingman himself, despite the brief experience in the surgical appliances factory that in the novel becomes Paul Morel's continued job. Chekhov said that the working-class writer purchases with his youth that which a more genteel writer is born with. But Lawrence gained everything, as a writer, from being brought up in the working class, and lost nothing by it. In *Sons and Lovers* he portrays the miners without idealizing them, as a socialist would; he relishes their human qualities (perhaps even a little jealously) and works them up as a subject for his art. He does not identify himself with them; his mother, too, we can be sure from the portrait of Mrs. Morel, tended to be somewhat aloof among the miners' wives. But Lawrence knows *as a writer* that he is related to working people, that he is bound up with them in the same order of physical and intimate existence, that it is workers' lives he has always looked on. Some of the most

affecting passages in this novel are based on the force and directness of working-class speech. "'E's niver gone, child?" Morel says
to his son when William dies. Paul answers in "educated" and even
prissy English, but the voice of the mines, the fields and the
kitchens is rendered straight and unashamed. Lawrence, who knew
how much he had lost as a man by siding with his mother in the
conflict, describes the miner Morel getting his own breakfast,
sitting "down to an hour of joy," with an irresistible appreciation
of the physical and human picture involved: "He toasted his bacon
on a fork and caught the drops of fat on his bread; then he put the
rasher on his thick slice of bread, and cut off chunks with a clasp-
knife, poured his tea into his saucer, and was happy."

The writer alone in Lawrence redeemed the weaknesses of
being too much his mother's son. We see the common round of
life among the miners' families very much as the young Lawrence
must have seen it, with the same peculiar directness. His mental
world was startlingly without superfluities and wasted motions.
What he wrote, he wrote. The striking sense of authority, of inner
conviction, that he associated with his mother's love gave him a
cutting briskness with things he disapproved. But this same
immediacy of response, when it touched what he loved, could
reach the greatest emotional depths. The description of William
Morel's coffin being carried into the house is a particular example
of this. "The coffin swayed, the men began to mount the three
steps with their load. Annie's candle flickered, and she whimpered
as the first men appeard, and the limbs and bowed heads of six
men struggled to climb into the room, bearing the coffin that rode
like sorrow on their living flesh." Lawrence's power to move the
reader lies in this ability to summon up all the physical attributes
associated with an object; he puts you into direct contact with all
its properties *as* an object. Rarely has the realistic novelist's need
to *present,* to present vividly, continually, and at the highest pitch
of pictorial concentration—the gift which has made the novel the
supreme literary form of modern times—rarely has this reached
such intense clarity of representation as it does in *Sons and Lovers.*
There are passages, as in Tolstoy, that make you realize what a loss
to directness of vision our increasing self-consciousness in literature represents. Lawrence is still face to face with life, and he can
describe the smallest things with the most attentive love and respect.

Lawrence does not describe, he would not attempt to describe, the object as in *itself* it really is. The effect of his prose
is always to heighten our consciousness of something, to relate it

to ourselves. He is a romantic—and in this book is concerned with the most romantic possible subject for a novelist, the growth of the writer's own consciousness. Yet he succeeded as a novelist, he succeeded brilliantly, because he was convinced that the novel is the great literary form, for no other could reproduce so much of the actual motion or "shimmer" of life, especially as expressed in the relationships between people. Since for Lawrence the great subject of literature was not the writer's own consciousness but consciousness between people, the living felt relationship between them, it was his very concern to represent the "shimmer" of life, the "wholeness"—these could have been mere romantic slogans—that made possible his brilliance as a novelist. He was to say, in a remarkable essay called "Why The Novel Matters," that "Only in the novel are *all* things given full play, or at least, they may be given full play, when we realize that life itself, and not inert safety, is the reason for living. For out of the full play of all things emerges the only thing that is anything, the wholeness of a man, the wholeness of a woman, man alive, and live woman." It was *relationship* that was sacred to him, as it was the relationships *with* his mother, her continuing presence in his mind and life, that gave him the sense of authority on which all his power rested. And as a novelist in *Sons and Lovers* he was able to rise above every conventional pitfall in an autobiographical novel by centering his whole vision on character as the focus of a relationship, not as an absolute.

After *Sons and Lovers,* which was his attempt to close up the past, Lawrence was to move on to novels like *The Rainbow* (1915) and *Women In Love* (1920), where the "non-human in humanity" was to be more important to him than "the old-fashioned human element." The First World War was to make impossible for Lawrence his belief in the old "stable ego" of character. Relationships, as the continuing interest of life, became in these more "problematical," less "conventional" novels, a version of man's general relationship, as an unknown in himself, to his unexplained universe. But the emphasis on growth and change in *Sons and Lovers,* the great book that closes Lawrence's first period, is from the known to the unknown; as Frank O'Connor has said, the book begins as a nineteenth century novel and turns into a twentieth century one. Where autobiographical novels with a "sensitive" artist or novelist as hero tend to emphasize the hero's growth to self-knowledge, the history of his "development," the striking thing about *Sons and Lovers,* and an instance of the creative mind behind it, is that it does not hand the "laurels of victory" to the hero. It does not allow him any self-sufficient victory over his circumstances. With the

greatest possible vividness it shows Paul Morel engulfed in relationships—with the mother he loves all too sufficiently, with the
"spiritual" Miriam and Clara, neither of whom he can love whole-
heartedly—relationships that are difficult and painful, and that
Lawrence leaves arrested in their pain and conflict. When Jessie
Chambers said of the first draft of *Sons and Lovers* that "Lawrence
had carried the situation to the point of deadlock and had stopped
there," she may have been right enough about it as an aborted
novel. But Lawrence's primary interest and concern as a novelist,
his sense of the continuing *flow* of relationship between people,
no matter how unclear and painful, no matter how far away it was
from the "solution" that the people themselves may have longed
for, is what makes this whole last section of the novel so telling.

But of course it is the opening half of *Sons and Lovers* that
makes the book great. The struggle between husband and wife
is described with a direct, unflinching power. Lawrence does not
try to bring anything to a psychological conclusion. The marriage
is a struggle, a continuing friction, a relationship where the wife's
old desire for her husband can still flash up through her resentment
of his "lowness." That is why everything in the "common round"
can be described with such tenderness, for the relationship of husband and wife sweeps into its unconscious passion everything that
the young Lawrence loved, and was attached to. Living in a mining
village on the edge of old Sherwood Forest, always close to the
country, Lawrence was as intimate with nature as any country
poet could have been, but he was lucky to see rural England and
the industrial Midlands in relation to each other; the country
soothed his senses, but a job all day long in a Nottingham factory
making out orders for surgical appliances did not encourage
nature worship. "On the fallow land the young wheat shone silkily.
Minton pit waved its plumes of white steam, coughed, and rattled
hoarsely." Lawrence is a great novelist of landscape, for he is concerned with the relationships of people living on farms, or walking
out into the country after the week's work in the city. He does not
romanticize nature, he describes it in its minute vibrations. In *Sons
and Lovers* the emotional effect of the "lyrical" passages depends
on Lawrence's extraordinary ability to convey movement and
meaning even in non-human things. But in this book nature never
provides evasion of human conflict and is not even a projection of
human feelings; it is the physical world that Lawrence grew up in,
and includes the pit down which a miner must go every day. Paul
in convalescence, sitting up in bed, would "see the fluffy horses
feeding at the troughs in the field, scattering their hay on the trod-

den yellow snow; watch the miners troop home—small, black figures trailing slowly in gangs across the white field."

This miniature, exquisite as a Japanese watercolor, is typical
of *Sons and Lovers*—the country lives and seethes, but it has no
mystical value. It is the landscape of Nottinghamshire and Derby-
shire, and in the book it is still what it was to Lawrence growing
up in it, an oasis of refreshment in an industrial world. The
countryside arouses young lovers to their buried feelings and it
supplies images for the "quickness," the vital current of relationship, that Lawrence valued most in life. It is never sacred in itself.
When you consider that this novel came out in 1913, at the height
of the "Georgian" period, when so many young poets of Lawrence's generation were mooning over nature, it is striking that *his*
chief interest is always the irreducible ambiguity of human relationships. Lawrence's language, in certain key scenes, certainly
recalls the emotional inflation of fiction in the "romantic" heyday
preceding the First World War. But the style is actually exalted
rather then literary. There is an unmistakably scriptural quality
to Lawrence's communication of extreme human feeling. Mr. Morel secretly cut young William's hair, and Mrs. Morel feels that "this
act of masculine clumsiness was the spear through the side of her
love." The Lawrences were Congregationalist, like American Puri-
tans. They were close to the Lord. The strong sense of himself
that Lawrence was always to have, the conviction that what he
felt was always terribly important just in the way he felt it, is im-
parted to Mrs. Morel herself in the great scene in which the in-
sulted husband, dizzy with drink, locks her out of the house. The
description of Mrs. Morel's feelings is charged with a kind of
frenzy of concern for her; the language sweeps from pole to pole
of feeling. Mrs. Morel is pregnant, and her sense of her moral
aloneness at this moment is overwhelming. "Mrs. Morel, scared
with passion, shivered to find herself out there in a great white
light, that fell cold on her, and gave a shock to her inflamed soul."
Later we read that "After a time the child, too, melted with her in
the mixing-pot of moonlight, and she rested with the hills and
lilies and houses, all swum together in a kind of swoon."

In this key scene of the mother's "trouble" (which must have
been based on things that Lawrence later heard from his mother),
the sense we get of Mrs. Morel, humiliated and enraged but in her
innermost being haughtily inviolate, gives us a sense of all the
power that Lawrence connected with his mother and of the power
in the relationship that flowed between them. In *Sons and Lovers*
he was able to re-create, for all time, the moment when the sym-

pathetic bond between them reached its greatest intensity—and
the moment when her death broke it. Ever after, Lawrence was
to try to re-create this living bond, this magic sympathy, between
himself and life. He often succeeded in creating an exciting and
fruitful version of it—in relationship to his extraordinary wife
Frieda; to a host of friends, disciples, admires and readers throughout the world; even to his own novels and stories, essays and
articles and poems and letters. Unlike Henry James, James Joyce,
Marcel Proust, T. S. Eliot, Lawrence always makes you feel that
not art but the quality of the lived experience is his greatest concern. That is why it is impossible to pick up anything by him without feeling revivified. Never were a writer's works more truly an
allegory of his life, and no other writer of his imaginative standing
has in our time written books that are so open to life.

Colin Clarke

Reductive Energy in The Rainbow

In *The Rainbow* as in Lawrence's work at large, the vitalistic virtues—spontaneity, untamed energy, intensity of being, power—
are endorsed elaborately. But the endorsement is noticeably
more ambiguous on some occasions than on others. The vitality
of the young Will Brangwen (he reminds Anna "of some animal,
some mysterious animal that lived in the darkness under the leaves
and never came out, but which lived vividly, swift and intense")
is one thing; the vitality that Will and Anna eventually release in
themselves in their bouts of natural-unnatural sensuality is
another. So for that matter is Ursula's fierce salt-burning corrosiveness under the moon, or the corrupt African potency of Skrebensky. In the one instance life is affirmed directly, positively, un-
ambiguously, if also with potential ferocity and violence—but
in the other instances reductively, in disintegration or corruption.

Here then, one would have thought, is a distinction of some
thematic importance; yet, curiously, the final effect of the novel
is to play the distinction down. The power of the horses which
threaten and terrify Ursula in the last chapter is, we sense, significantly different from the corrosive menace of Ursula herself in
the moonlight, and we feel that somehow the difference ought to
tell in the story; yet nothing is made of it. It is of course a differ-
ence-in-similarity. In each case we are concerned with the menace
of power in unmitigated assertion and it has in fact been argued,
by H. M. Daleski, that Ursula's traumatic adventure recapitulates
symbolically the decisive moments in her soul's journey, re-enact-
ing her past surrenders to "the anarchy of elemental passion."
But although, positioned as it is, the episode would appear to make
some claim to summational significance, the claim is in fact only
partially substantiated. If indeed, as Daleski has argued, the "pressing, pressing, pressing" of the horses refers us back to the sort of
assertion to which Ursula herself had resorted with Skrebensky,
a frenetic assertion of her feminine self in the endeavor to burst
free to fulness of being, it must still be said that there is a great
deal in her relationship with her lover to which the episode, so in-

From The River of Dissolution *by Colin Clarke. Routledge & Kegan Paul
Ltd., 1969. Reprinted by permission.*

33

terpreted, has no relevance. For what has this display of massive equine power to do with the explosive life-affirmation of the Ursula who most lives in our imaginations, the corrosive-disinte-grative Ursula whose affirmation of life is at the same time a re-duction of life? And after all it is this paradoxical Ursula who is the growing point as well as the strength of the novel in its latter phases; it is she who points forward most emphatically to *Women in Love.*

Moreover, Ursula's corrosiveness is anticipated by her father's; the one story has its roots deep in the other. So if the significance of the later story is not caught up adequately into the final chapter, the same is true, inevitably, of the earlier one. It is the *recurrent* exploration into the reductive processes that, more than anything else, gives continuity and shape to the novel; and by the same token it is the failure to realize the full cumulative signi-ficance of the discoveries made in the course of that exploration that does most to account for one's sense, toward the end, of a richness of meaning that has not altogether found its proper form. This at any rate is the case I propose to argue in the present chap-ter. "The novel is the highest example of subtle inter-relatedness that man has discovered," Lawrence was to claim later. It is just this interrelatedness that we find wanting, too often, in the latter half of *The Rainbow.*

In the chapter "Anna Victrix" we remark the partial emer-gence of a syndrome of images that was to prove crucial in the articulation of the reductive theme in *Women in Love;* and no passage is more prophetic than the following, with its ambiguous stress on enforced *downward* movement.

> At first she went on blithely enough with him shut down beside her. But then his spell began to take hold of her. The dark, seething potency of him, the power of a creature that lies hidden and exerts its will to the destruction of the free-running creature, as the tiger ly-ing in the darkness of the leaves steadily enforces the fall and death of the light creatures that drink by the waterside in the morning, gradually began to take effect on her. Though he lay there in his darkness and did not move, yet she knew he lay waiting for her. She felt his will fastening on her and pulling her down, even whilst he was silent and obscure.
>
> She found that, in all her outgoings and her incomings, he pre-vented her. Gradually she realized that she was being borne down by him, borne down by the clinging, heavy weight of him, that he was pulling her down as a leopard clings to a wild cow and exhausts her and pulls her down. . . .
>
> . . . Why did he want to drag her down, and kill her spirit? Why

did he want to deny her spirit? Why did he deny her spirituality, hold her for a body only? And was he to claim her carcase? . . . "What do you do to me?" she cried. . . . "There is something horrible in you, something dark and beastly in your will."

Will's reductive activity is potent, vital, sanctioned by Nature (assimilated, that is, to the splendid destructiveness of leopards and tigers) but also debilitating, *un*-natural, monstrous. The downward tug is a degradation, an obscenity: "And was he to claim her carcase?" Whether Will is "actually" as monstrous as he seems to Anna is not of course a critical issue. There is no way of going behind the words themselves to unverbalized facts, and what the words present us with is something like an antinomy—a vision of horror and perversity imposed, immediately, upon a no less cogent vision of potency and life. What we carry away is an impression not so much of complexity of "character" as of the value-and-cost of living within the darkness.

And the same is true of the way Will's impressively rendered sensuality is directly overlaid by his agonizing sense of vacuity and dependence; he is extremely vulnerable, and at the same time powerful. This point needs to be labored a little, because of the way the dependence and weakness have been dwelt upon in critical commentaries and the potency correspondingly ignored. Of the potency we are assured again and again:

> There was something thick, dark, dense, powerful about him that irritated her too deeply for her to speak of it.

or:

> And ever and again he appeared as the dread flame of power. Sometimes, when he stood in the doorway, his face lit up, he seemed like an Annunciation to her, her heart beat fast. And she watched him, suspended. He had a dark, burning being that she dreaded and resisted.

Yet Daleski permits himself to remark that Will is "the weak, if not quite the broken, end of the arch"; and he concludes that the conflict between Will and Anna "derives, ultimately, from *his* imperfections." One wonders then how it is that Anna should come in time to sustain herself with her husband's subterranean strength:

> She learned not to dread and to hate him, but to fill herself with him, to give herself to his black, sensual power, that was hidden all the daytime.

On the other hand we are not allowed to forget that the power Will
mediates in the darkness is paid for by an acquaintance with the
terrors of the darkness—and the obscenities too.

> She wanted to desert him, to leave him a prey to the open, with the
> unclean dogs of the darkness setting on to devour him. He must beat
> her, and make her stay with him.

In the paragraph immediately preceding we find this:

> And, at the bottom of her soul, she felt he wanted her to be dark,
> unnatural. Sometimes, when he seemed like the darkness covering
> and smothering her, she revolted almost in horror, and struck at him.

Will is terrified of the unclean creatures of the dark; yet in Anna's
eyes he is one of those creatures himself, potent, sinister, horrify-
ing. In short, what at one moment is potency becomes at the next,
with a sudden shift of perspective, vulnerability. Nor are terror and
horror absolute qualities—or static; they create, or convert themselves into their opposites *"Because* she dreaded him and held
him in horror, he became wicked, he wanted to destroy"; "And
he began to shudder. . . . He must beat her, and make her stay
with him." In both Will and Anna power is a function of vulnerability and vulnerability of power.
The potency and the capacity for degradation—the fear of the
night and the splendid dark sensuality—belong to a single individual, and what is being deviously suggested is that the potency
can't be had *without* the degradation. The more sophisticated
strategy of *Women in Love* is already within sight.

If the endorsement of reductive power in "Anna Victrix" is
largely oblique, by the time we reach the chapter "The Child"
it has become explicit, though not, for that reason, unambiguous.
First there is the account of Will's unconsummated seduction of
the young girl he meets in Nottingham. A moralistic interpretation
of this scene, entailing a simple ethical judgment on Will's perversity and pursuit of sensation for its own sake, would drastically
impoverish its significance.

> He did not care about her, except that he wanted to overcome her
> resistance, to have her in his power, fully and exhaustively to enjoy
> her.

This and similar passages, taken out of context, could be used to

support the view that the whole episode points the distance between a fully human sexuality and the aridness of unassimilated
desire.

> Just his own senses were supreme. All the rest was external, insignif-
> icant, leaving him alone with this girl whom he wanted to absorb,
> whose properties he wanted to absorb into his own senses. . . .
> But he was patiently working for her relaxation, patiently, his whole
> being fixed in the smile of latent gratification, his whole body electric
> with a subtle, powerful, reducing force upon her.

Yet this premediated sensuality (one notes how often Lawrence
resorts to the image of electricity to suggest the *frisson* of white
or sensational sex) opens up for Will a new world of Absolute
Beauty.

> And his hand that grasped her side felt one curve of her, and it
> seemed like a new creation to him, a reality, an absolute, an existing
> tangible beauty of the absolute.

Clearly, the human value of Will's experience is by no means
easily determined. Indeed its final value *cannot* be determined;
the effect of Lawrence's art is to discourage in the reader any
tendency to reach a single and ready-defined judgment. The destruction of the flesh in conscious sensuality is presented very
deliberately for contemplation, as though the intention were to
invite a dismissive moral judgment; but, just as deliberately, any
such judgment is held at bay. The perversity and destructiveness
are fully conceded and, artistically, fully realized; but so is the
beauty, the "amazing beauty and pleasure." As so often in Lawrence's work the effect is one of double exposure: we register the
impulse to destruction even while we acknowledge the enhance-
ment of life.

These complexities and tensions are sustained and indeed
intensified in the sequence that follows when Will, returning home,
incites Anna to a new kind of love-making, "a sensuality violent
and extreme as death."

> There was no tenderness, no love between them any more, only the
> maddening, sensuous lust for discovery and the insatiable, exorbitant
> gratification in the sensual beauties of her body. . . .
> They accepted shame, and were one with it in their most unlicensed
> pleasures. It was incorporated. It was a bud that blossomed into
> beauty and heavy, fundamental gratification.

... What we observe first and foremost is that the new licentiousness has an absolute, or non-instrumental, value. Obviously (for the language is quite explicit) Will's sensuality is disintegrative. A deliberate, piece-meal exploitation of the body takes the place of tenderness and love. Yet this disintegrative sex is now discovered to be a way-in to life, and, above all, a revelation of beauty, "supreme, immoral, Absolute Beauty." This is the bold truth we are required to confront. . . . It is the final paragraphs of the chapter that . . . we find ourselves in a more reassuring, not to say cozy world, where social purposiveness is triumphant and even lust turns (eventually) a moral mill.

> He wanted to be unanimous with the whole of purposive mankind. . . . For the first time he began to take real interest in a public affair. He had at length, from his profound sensual activity, developed a real purposive self.

The *rapprochement* effected between the reductive and the creative in these last paragraphs impresses one as willed and glib, indeed as largely unreal. We are not to be convinced by mere assertion that social purposiveness can develop out of sensuality and a profound moral indifference; this, surely, is something that calls for patient demonstration.

On the other hand the "mere assertion" was in itself an achievement; Lawrence was breaking new ground, even if he was doing so at a purely discursive level. To gauge the distance, as it were, between the "argument" of the paragraphs under review and the "argument" of the paragraphs that conclude the preceding chapter, "The Cathedral," is one way of enforcing this point.

> He still remained motionless, seething with inchoate rage, when his whole nature seemed to disintegrate. He seemed to live with a strain upon himself, and occasionally came these dark, chaotic rages, the lust for destruction. She then fought with him, and their fights were horrible, murderous. And then the passion between them came just as black and awful. . . .
> He made himself a woodwork shed, in which to restore things which were destroyed in the church. So he had plenty to do: his wife, his child, the church, the woodwork, and his wage-earning, all occupying him. If only there were not some limit to him, some darkness across his eyes! . . . He was unready for fulfilment. Something undeveloped in him, there was a darkness in him which he *could* not unfold, which would never unfold in him.

This might well seem to be more honest than the conclusion to the chapter that follows; for Will's lust for destruction, of which we have heard so much and which we now recognize as a basic fact about him, is not lost sight of at all, even while we are being assured of his constructiveness and purposiveness. In other words, the creative and the reductive co-exist throughout; the one is not simply *substituted* for the other, as in the later passage, which seems by comparison a good deal too smooth. On the other hand the theme of the later passage is intrinsically more "difficult." Whereas in the earlier instance Will's creativeness and destructiveness, if undissociated are also causally unconnected, in the later instance it is actually *from* the destructiveness (in this case disintegrative sensuality) that the creativeness, we are to believe, proceeds, or develops. In cold fact however, the total failure to dramatize this development means that the destructive and the creative seem no more inwardly affiliated than they were in the earlier sequence. Indeed less so; virtually they lose contact.

And it is a loss of contact of just this kind that we frequently remark in the remaining chapters. The story repeatedly concerns itself with disintegration and destructiveness; and we can scarcely fail to assume, as we proceed, that it will be part of this concern to discover and define a significant pattern of relationships between *kinds* of disintegration: *this* disintegrative process will prove to have a bearing on *that.* But in the event no such pattern emerges; "cross-reference" seems both to be encouraged and not encouraged. There is the fiercely corrosive and violently destructive activity of Ursula in the moonlight; there is the corruption and social disintegration at Wiggiston, and the corresponding despair of Ursula herself—("She had no connexion with other people. Her lot was isolated and deadly. There was nothing for her anywhere, but this black disintegration"); there is the splendid-sinister potency of Skrebensky, corrupt, fecund, destructive ("He kissed her, and she quivered as if she were being destroyed, shattered"); and there is Ursula's vision of advancing corruption at the very end of the novel. But to what extent these kinds of disintegration bear upon each other is not clear. Whereas in *Women in Love* the densely reticulated imagery is constantly persuading us to see identities in difference, to make discriminations and discover analogies, in the latter part of *The Rainbow* we seem to be invited teasingly to embark on this same procedure only in the end to be frustrated.

But these judgments require substantiating and I turn first

to the scene, in the chapter "First Love," in which the adolescent Ursula annihilates her lover under the moon. Once again (as in the case of Will Brangwen, "the sensual male seeking his pleasure") we find ourselves acknowledging a value in activity patently opposed to the creative and integrative. "But hard and fierce she had fastened upon him, cold as the moon and burning as a fierce salt . . . seething like some cruel, corrosive salt." "Cold . . . and burning": the oxymoron (a common one wherever Lawrence is concerned with the reductive processes) focuses the sense of an inverse vitality running counter to growth and to warm organic blood desire. Nowhere in the novel is human personality reduced more obviously and more drastically to the inhuman and inorganic, and yet nowhere are we more aware of power and energy humanly mediated. The recurrent images—moonlight, steel, corrosive salt, the sea—exclude the organic entirely, and one thinks of the famous letter on Marinetti and the Futurists (5 June, 1914):

> . . . it is the inhuman will, call if physiology, or like Marinetti—physiology of matter, that fascinates me. I don't so much care about what the woman *feels*—in the ordinary usage of the word. That presumes an *ego* to feel with. . . . You mustn't look in my novel for the old stable *ego* of the character.

In a stimulating article on *The Narrative Technique of "The Rainbow"* Roger Sale has considered the literary means by which Lawrence contrived to "break down 'the old stable ego of character.'" It is not so much Sale's argument itself that concerns me here as the significance of that metaphor of "breaking down."

> The simplest declarative sentence is one of the main aids the novelist has in building up a stable ego, an identity. . . .
> If we turn to a passage in *The Rainbow,* we can show how Lawrence tries there to break down this natural building-up process. . . .

The phrasing could not be more apt—or revealing; for "breaking down" is a common Laurentian synonym for "reduction." So Sale pays his tribute unconsciously to the iconic power of Lawrence's art, and demonstrates indirectly that the major novels are about the reductive process not only in the most obvious or literal sense but in the further sense that they themselves image that process. In the episode under review we remark how the fiercely corrosive activity of the fictive Ursula is matched, and to that extent endorsed, by the corrosive activity—no less vigorous—of the artist himself. And this endorsement goes far toward explaining why our moral sense should fail to be outraged by Ursula's enormous wilfulness." Her attitude to Skrebensky is inhuman, but then so is the novelist's art, in the sense that part of what he is engaged in is the reduction of human personality to an inhuman or material substratum. But this involves no diminishing of artistic intensity; indeed it has the reverse effect, and the novelist creates a notable artificial beauty—a beauty "immoral and against mankind."

Probably the best gloss on these pages is a passage . . . from *The Crown*. (It is a passage significant also for the kind of bearing it does *not* have on the episode or on the novel generally . . .)

> Leonardo knew this: he knew the strange endlessness of the flux of corruption. It is Mona Lisa's ironic smile. Even Michael Angelo knew it. It is in his *Leda and the Swan*. For the swan is one of the symbols of divine corruption with its reptile feet buried in the ooze and mud, its voluptuous form yielding and embracing the ooze of water, its beauty white and cold and terrifying, like the dead beauty of the moon, like the water-lily, the sacred lotus, its neck and head like the snake, it is for us a flame of the cold white fire of flux, the phosphorescence of corruption, the salt, cold burning of the sea which corrodes all it touches, coldly reduces every sun-built form to ash, to the original elements. This is the beauty of the swan, the lotus, the snake, this cold white salty fire of infinite reduction. And there was some suggestion of this in the Christ of the early Chritians, the Christ who was the Fish.

The paradoxes are a good deal sharper in the novel than in the essay (with the exception of that last equation of Christ and Fish), for the obvious reason that Ursula, a human being, is further removed than snake or swan from "the original elements," so that in the novel the reductive process is that much more spectacular. For all that, we are not more interested in the morality of Ursula's behavior, essentially, than we would be in the behavior of swan or snake. Or, to make the point perhaps less provocatively, we are interested in the morality of her behavior only to the extent that we are interested in her dehumanization. It is relevant to recall that remarkable passage in E. T.'s memoir where an account is given of three occasions on which Lawrence became wildly distraught—possessed—under the combined influence of moonlight and sea:

> I was really frightened then—not physically, but deep in my soul. He created an atmosphere not of death which after all is part of

mortality, but of an utter negation of life, as though he had become dehumanized.

Analogously, in the scene in *The Rainbow,* one is impressed not so much by Ursula's will to separateness, or her frenetic feminine assertiveness, though these qualities are doubtless evident enough, as by her intimidating inhuman-ness.[1] Yet the further she departs from the warmly living the more evidence she gives of vitality of a different kind—inverse, disintegrative. Inverse is Birkin's word; and indeed his notion of "inverse process" is loosely relevant to the whole episode.

> When the stream of synthetic creation lapses, we find ourselves part of the inverse process, the blood of destructive creation. Aphrodite is born in the first spasm of universal dissolution—then the snakes and swans and lotus—marsh-flowers—and Gudrun and Gerald—born in the process of destructive creation. . . . It is a progressive process—and it ends in universal nothing. . . .

The process can end only in a re-assimilation to the anonymous energies of nature; yet it is productive of a deadly and distinctive beauty. And in *The Rainbow,* likewise, beauty is a product of the reductive process, a function of reductive power.

> She stood for some moments out in the overwhelming luminosity of the moon. She seemed a beam of gleaming power. She was afraid of what she was. Looking at him, at his shadowy, unreal, wavering presence a sudden lust seized her, to lay hold of him and tear him and make him into nothing. Her hands and wrists felt immeasurably hard and strong, like blades.

This revelation of life and beauty where we might scarcely be supposed to expect it, in a process that brutally affronts our sympathies—in a progressive departure from the human—is what the episode is centrally about. (It is for the most part a fully realized rhetorical beauty and rhetorical life, though there is, surely, some overwriting.) To identify with Ursula's daytime consciousness, and accept as self-validating the slow horror she experiences as

---

[1] The de-humanizing process is associated with the salt sea in the Melville essay too:

> Away, away from humanity. To the sea. The naked salt,
> elemental sea. To go to sea, to escape humanity.
> The human heart gets into a frenzy at last, in its desire to
> dehumanize itself. *(final version)*

she gradually recovers herself (as one critic has done) is clearly inappropriate. Primarily, Ursula's horror is there to measure the recession of the magical and mythic. There is no suggestion that the familiar order of reality is the more valid or true; it is simply different.

And indeed the sheer fact of difference is stated as cogently as could well be. It is a question however whether the statement is not in fact too cogent. I have suggested, apropos of the final paragraphs of the chapter "The Child," that Lawrence's task is to communicate a sense of the distinction between pure creation and destructive creation—or the vital and the perversely vital—without effecting a simple dissociation between them. In the earlier sequences involving Tom and Lydia, and Anna and Will, the constant modulation from the mythic to the commonplace, and vice versa, has established the existence of a consciousness at once distinct from our familiar daytime consciousness and at the same time prone to assert itself in the context of daytime living. Will's murderously reductive activity in the chapter "Anna Victrix" is a quality of his everyday behavior and also the utterance of a self that can seem at moments extravagantly alien. But from the stackyard scene on there is a tendency for the magical and the everyday—the subterranean self and the social self—to move apart. And the abrupt dissociation of personae at the end of the scene, when Ursula repudiates her "corrosive self" with horror (while the night is suddenly "struck back into its old, accustomed, mild reality") is, in this connection, only too suggestive of what is to come. A truth is enforced, but at the expense of a counter-truth; Ursula's ruthless energy is made to seem *merely* alien.

It is Skrebensky's character however that tends most conspicuously to bifurcate, and in a way that bears even more suggestively on my argument. If it is a mistake to interpret Ursula's lurid behavior under the moon with a moralistic bias, it is a parallel mistake to ignore the corrupt vitality of her lover and to write him off as a hollow man *simpliciter*. Leavis has perhaps led the way here; at any rate he has concerned himself exclusively with Skrebensky's shortcomings, laying stress upon his "good-citizen acceptance of the social function as the ultimate meaning of life" and pointing to the connection between this acceptance and his "inadequacy as a lover." Others, designedly or not, have followed suit. S. L. Goldberg lumps Skrebensky with Winifred Inger and Tom Brangwen, "the irrevocably lost." Daleski, quoting the argument between Ursula and Skrebensky about being a soldier, comments:

This passage establishes not only that Skrebensky is "not exactly" a soldier, but that he is not exactly anything. If, unlike Will, he does not deny the outside world, he accepts his place in it with a mechanical and unadventurous complacency. . . .
Skrebensky is even less defined as a man than either Tom or Will; lacking the rooted stability of the one and the passionate aspiration of the other, he has no real identity.

But what of the Skrebensky who, like Ursula herself, can be a vehicle of intense vitality, positive reductive, potent, corrupt?

> He talked to her all the while in low tones about Africa, conveying something strange and sensual to her: the negro, with his loose, soft passion that could envelop one like a bath. Gradually he transferred to her the hot, fecund darkness that possessed his own blood. He was strangely secret. The whole world must be abolished. . . .
>
> He seemed like the living darkness upon her, she was in the embrace of the strong darkness. He held her enclosed, soft, unutterably soft, and with the unrelaxing softness of fate, the relentless softness of fecundity. . . .
>
> It was bliss, it was the nucleolating of the fecund darkness. Once the vessel had vibrated till it was shattered, the light of consciousness gone, then the darkness reigned, and the unutterable satisfaction.

Here again is that effect of double exposure to which I have already alluded: on the one hand an impression of cultural and organic regression, on the other hand the sensual transfiguration, "the unutterable satisfaction." It is the familiar paradox:

> "Corruption will at last break down for us the deadened forms, and release us into the infinity."

The image of the turgid African night is parallel to those other images of potency-in-disintegration, the flaring moon and the salt-burning sea. Skrebensky's sensuality is at once reductive, regressive, a breaking down ("One breathes it, like a smell of blood," "The whole world must be abolished") and a release into infinity. The sensual ecstasy has its roots in corruption. The lovers inhabit an "unblemished darkness"; yet the matrix (as it were) of this darkness is that other, sinister darkness of Africa. This latter is the darkness that sustains them, ultimately—as the swan has its reptile feet buried in the ooze and mud. We are in the world of *Women in Love*. The teeming night is recognizably Birkin's "dark river of dissolution": "massive and *fluid* with terror," "his loose, soft passion that could envelop one like a *bath*," "they walked the darkness beside the massive *river*," "the soft *flow* of his kiss, . . . the warm fecund flow of his kiss," "one fecund nucleus of the *fluid* darkness." This is very obviously in the spirit of the later novel. It anticipates Birkin's *"fountain* of mystic corruption."

Yet the Ursula-Skrebensky story, it is commonly agreed, is not, by a long way, as coherent or compelling as for the most part the story of *Women in Love* is. And one reason at least is plain. The final movement of *The Rainbow* is organized around a single human relationship. Inevitably this deprives Lawrence of the scope he needed for elaborating those paradoxical themes which, all the evidence goes to show, were now so deeply engaging his imagination. It is no accident that the single pair of lovers became two pairs of lovers in the sequel; they had to. Skrebensky is called on to discharge the functions of both Birkin *and* Gerald to "figure," in Jamesian phrase, the possibilities both for life *and* death in reductive sexuality. Not surprisingly he proves unequal to the task. At a non-narrative level the paradox about living disintegration can be developed and protracted as far as ingenuity will allow; but at the narrative level the limits to this process are stricter. *The Rainbow* is a novel, with a story. Skrebensky cannot, in the story, be given over finally to disintegration and also be redeemed. And, in the event, under these novelistic pressures his character falls apart into *two* characters.

On the one hand there is Skrebensky the darkly potent lover, inhabitant of the fecund universal night.

> Everything he did was a voluptuous pleasure to him—either to ride on horseback, or to walk, or to lie in the sun, or to drink in a public-house. He had no use for people, nor for words. He had an amused pleasure in everything, a great sense of voluptuous richness in himself. . . .

There is little doubt that we are to accept this vitality as real. Moreover it entails a certain correlative distinction at a more personal and conscious level.

> She took him home, and he stayed a week-end at Beldover with her family. She loved having him in the house. Strange how he seemed to come into the atmosphere of her family, with his laughing, insidious grace. They all loved him, he was kin to them. His raillery, his warm, voluptuous mocking presence was meat and joy to the Brangwen household. For this house was always quivering with darkness, they put off their puppet form when they came home, to lie and drowse in the sun.

The emphasis here is still on the dark under-life; yet laughing insidious grace, raillery, warmth and voluptuous mockery also suggest less esoteric qualities—more "human" and social—and a corresponding fullness or completeness of being. At any rate we are left in no doubt of the richness and abundance of life which the relationship with Skrebensky, for all its limitations, does release. The lovers are held together *only* in the sensual subconsciousness, yet that only includes so much.

> Then he turned and kissed her, and she waited for him. The pain to her was the pain she wanted, the agony was the agony she wanted. She was caught up, entangled in the powerful vibration of the night. The man, what was he?—a dark, powerful vibration that encompassed her. She passed away as on a dark wind, far, far away, into the pristine darkness of paradise, into the original immortality. She entered the dark fields of immortality.

In the face of this and similar passages it is scarcely adequate to say of Skrebensky that though he satisfies Ursula "time after time in their physical relations" he fails her at the last in the "'beyondness of sex' . . .—where Birkin in *Women in Love* will not fail with Ursula later." Something like this, it is true, is Ursula's own reading of the situation:

> The salt, bitter passion of the sea, its indifference to the earth, its swinging definite motion, its strength, its attack, and its salt burning, seemed to provoke her to a pitch of madness, tantalizing her with vast suggestions of fulfilment. And then, for personification, would come Skrebensky, Skrebensky, whom she knew, whom she was fond of, who was attractive, but whose soul could not contain her in its waves of strength, nor his breast compel her in burning, salty passion.

But we remember not only how she and Skrebensky had "stood together, dark, fluid, *infinitely* potent, giving the living lie to the dead whole which contained them" or had passed away "into the pristine darkness of paradise," or how "perfectly and supremely free" they were, "proud beyond all question, and *surpassing mortal conditions,*" but also the sinister African potency, the destructiveness and indifference to humanity which Skrebensky had darkly communicated and which, I have argued, are analogous to the "salt, bitter passion" which, we now learn, he is utterly deficient in.
    But then of course there is the other Skrebensky.

> His life lay in the established order of things. He had his five senses too. They were to be gratified. . . .

> The good of the greatest number was all that mattered. That which was the greatest good for them all, collectively, was the greatest good for the individual.

This is the Skrebensky the commentators have fixed upon—a vacuity; a mere social integer, essentially without identity and living in pure externality through the senses.

It is true that the contrast between the two Skrebenskys is not always as steep as the passages quoted might suggest. There are moments when the vacuity and the power live together convincingly, are accepted as belonging to a single person.

> He seemed so balanced and sure, he made such a confident presence. He was a great rider, so there was about him some of a horseman's sureness, and habitual definiteness of decision, also some of the horseman's animal darkness. Yet his soul was only the more wavering, vague. . . . She could only feel the dark, heavy fixity of his animal desire. . . . All must be kept so dark, the consciousness must admit nothing. . . . He was always side-tracking, always side-tracking his own soul. She could see him so well out there, in India—one of the governing class, superimposed upon an old civilisation, lord and master of a clumsier civilisation than his own.

Here Skrebensky's limitations are a believable aspect of his strength; the animal darkness, the fixity of animal desire, the disinclination to bring things to consciousness, the side-tracking of his own soul—this all hangs together. If his soul is wavering and vague, if he virtually has no soul, this is not because he lives purely in the senses, but because he has the inarticulateness of an animal—both its dark power and its heavy fixity.

And if Skrebensky's sensual being impresses us as far shallower on some occasions than on others, something similar is true of Ursula. She however is always exempted from adverse judgement.

> Yet she loved him, the body of him, whatever his decisions might be. . . . She caught his brilliant, burnished glamour. Her heart and her soul were shut away fast down below, hidden. She was free of them. She was to have her satisfaction.

We may compare this with the earlier comment on Skrebensky: "He had his five senses too. They were to be gratified." But whereas in the one instance dissociated sensuality releases a glow and splendor of life ("She became proud and erect, like a flower, putting itself forth in its proper strength") in the other it is a token of death ("Skrebensky, somehow, had created a deadness around her, a sterility, as if the world were ashes. . . . Why did he never really want a woman, not with the whole of him: never love, never worship, only just physically want her?) When Skrebensky finally fails Ursula at the end, they are engaged in a pursuit of just that kind of satisfaction which she herself had set up as a goal ("Her heart and soul were shut away. . . . She was to have her satisfaction"); yet responsibility for this failure seems to be laid exclusively at Skrebensky's door.

> She liked it, the electric fire of the silk under his hands upon her limbs. . . . Yet she did not feel beautiful. All the time, she felt she was not beautiful to him, only exciting. She let him take her, and he seemed mad, mad with excited passion. But she, as she lay afterwards on the cold, soft sand, looking up at the blotted, faintly luminous sky, felt that she was as cold now as she had been before.

The transfiguration in the flesh which Ursula had unquestionably enjoyed with Skrebensky is here repudiated, and the intoxication of the senses which they shared is conceived of as having ended in itself; it involved, apparently, "no connexion with the unknown." But the reader's recollections, as I have suggested, are different from Ursula's, and are not so rapidly erased.

One can conceive easily enough of an ending to the novel which would seem to resolve these warring tensions: Ursula, looking back in gratitude to the very real satisfaction and fulfilment Skrebensky had brought, might yet acknowledge that in the end the sensual ecstasy could not in itself sustain her. Yet, clearly, tensions as powerful as these are not to be resolved so neatly and rationally. For Lawrence is under an evident compulsion to make *incompatible* statements about voluptuousness or dissociated sensuality, and is struggling to find a novelistic pattern sufficiently flexible to allow him to do so. The pattern to which he is committed is transparently *not* sufficiently flexible; so we find him asserting of Skrebensky that his sensuality ends in sensuality and yet also that it leads into the unknown.

There is an essay of this period, *The Lemon Gardens* (it appeared in the *English Review* in September 1913),* in which this doubleness of attitude to self-conscious sensuality is articulated with especial clarity.

---

*This essay appeared later in *Twilight in Italy*. [*ed. note.*]

This is the soul of the Italian since the Renaissance. In the sunshine he basks asleep, gathering up a vintage into his veins which in the night-time he will distil into ecstatic sensual delight, the intense, white-cold ecstasy of darkness and moonlight, the raucous, cat-like, destructive enjoyment, the senses conscious and crying out in their consciousness in the pangs of the enjoyment, which has consumed the southern nation, perhaps all the Latin races, since the Renaissance. . . .

This is one way of transfiguration into the eternal flame, the transfiguration through ecstasy in the flesh. . . . And this is why the Italian is attractive, supple, and beautiful, because he worships the Godhead in the flesh. We envy him, we feel pale and insignificant beside him. Yet at the same time we feel superior to him, as if he were a child and we adult.

Wherein are we superior? Only because we went beyond the phallus in the search of the Godhead, the creative origin. And we found the physical forces and the secrets of science. . . .

But we have exhausted ourselves in the process. We have found great treasures, and we are now impotent to use them. So we have said: "What good are these treasures, they are vulgar nothings." We have said: "Let us go back from this adventuring, let us enjoy our own flesh, like the Italian." But our habit of life, our very constitution, prevents our being quite like the Italian. The phallus will never serve us as a Godhead, because we do not believe in it: no Northern race does. Therefore, either we set ourselves to serve our children, calling them "the future," or else we turn perverse and destructive, give ourselves joy in the destruction of the flesh.

"Perverse and destructive": the tone is distinctly unsympathetic. "This is one way of transfiguration into the eternal flame": the tone is far from unsympathetic. Yet the topic is essentially the same on each occasion. True, the Italian's worship of the Godhead in the flesh is genuine, whereas the northerner's is derivative and mechanical. Yet the theme in each instance is the self-consciousness of the flesh, destructive enjoyment, the pursuit of maximum sensation, the senses conscious and crying out in their consciousness. And these in effect are the ambiguities of the Ursula-Skrebensky story. We may compare:

> She vibrated like a jet of electric, firm fluid in response. Yet she did not feel beautiful. All the time, she felt she was not beautiful to him, only exciting.

And

> But the fire is cold, as in the eyes of a cat, it is a green fire. It is fluid, electric.

In the essay the cold fire has a splendor absent from the episode in the novel.

> This is the supremacy of the flesh, which devours all, and becomes transfigured into a magnificent brindled flame, a burning bush indeed.

But as I have suggested, a dismissive note—corresponding to the "not beautiful, . . . only exciting" of the novel—is there in the essay too, in the unsympathetic attitude to the northerner's merely mechanical sensation-hunting.

And so it is that the character of Skrebensky fails in the last analysis to cohere. He is made a butt, like the northerner, because he seeks the destruction of the flesh, or pure gratification through the senses; yet just the capacity to live through the flesh, reductively, like the Italian, is his strength. It is only with *Women in Love* that Lawrence finds for this teasing paradox an appropriate dramatic correlative.

In the passage from *The Crown* which I have chosen as epigraph to the second part of this book Lawrence lists various alternative modes of the activity of departure. These are decay, corruption, destruction, and breaking down; and elsewhere in the essay he supplies others—resolving down, reduction, corrosion, decomposition, dissolution, disintergration. In *Women in Love* these various processes—in all their ambiguity as opposite equivalents of creation—are represented comprehensively; but in *The Rainbow* much less so. Decay and corruption, crucial images in the later novel, play a minor and for the most part unobstrusive role in the earlier one; moreover their value or force is not on the whole ambiguous.[2] In the passage in which they are most obviously deployed—the account of Ursula's visit to Wiggiston with Winifred Inger—their significance is all on the surface and noticeably uncomplicated. The marsh, in *Women in Love* foul and deadly yet also a source of perverse but genuine vitality, is here merely foul and deadly. Or very nearly so.

> Her Uncle Tom too had something marshy about him—the succulent moistness and turgidity, and the same brackish, nauseating effect of a marsh, where life and decaying are one.

---

[2] I do not wish to suggest that there is an absolute and necessary virtue in ambiguity. It is true that my argument in this book seems to entail that proposition, but largely because I am concerned with one aspect only of Lawrence's art.

The nausea is absolute and uncomplicated, it would seem; yet even here there is a hint of the ambivalence to come.

> She too, Winifred, worshipped the impure abstraction, the mechanisms of matter. There, there, in the machine, in service of the machine, was she free from the clog and degradation of human feeling.

The notion that to be human is necessarily to be nourished in *corruption* ("clog and degradation") is well within sight here, so that a cross-reference to the dominant contextual image of the marsh at any rate *begins* to be set in motion: we seem to catch at some such implied significance as that the marsh, admittedly clogging and vile, is for all that, or rather all the more for that, a source of life. The resonance is faint and apparently accidental, but prophetic of *Women in Love,* without question.

In the handling of this theme of corruption in *The Rainbow* one is indeed haunted by a sense of half-realized significance. There is the treatment of Ursula's uncle Tom for instance. Before the meeting at Wiggiston he had already made a decisive impact upon her imagination, when she saw him at the farm after the drowning of his father.

> She could see him, in all his elegant demeanour, bestial, almost corrupt. And she was frightened. She never forgot to look for the bestial, frightening side of him, after this.
>
> He said "Good-bye" to his mother and went away at once. Ursula almost shrank from his kiss, now. She wanted it nevertheless, and the little revulsion as well.

And we remember this when he appears next, at the wedding (the passage is too long to quote in full).

> A kind of flame of physical desire was gradually beating up in the Marsh. . . . Tom Brangwen, with all his secret power, seemed to fan the flame that was rising. . . .
>
> The music began, and the bond began to slip. Tom Brangwen was dancing with the bride, quick and fluid and as if in another element, inaccessible as the creatures that move in the water. . . . One couple after another was washed and absorbed into the deep underwater of the dance.
>
> "Come," said Ursula to Skrebensky, laying her hand on his arm. . . .

> It was his will and her will locked in a trance of motion, two wills
> locked in one motion, yet never fusing, never yielding one to the
> other. It was a glaucous, intertwining, delicious flux and contest in
> flux.

The dichotomies of the moralist are hopelessly irrelevant here.
The underworld over which the half-sinister Tom Brangwen pre-
sides is a place of dangerous licence, of enchancement, of heightened life, a place for privileged to enter. Yet if here, in his equivocal way, Tom releases life, and later, at Wiggiston, is an un-
equivocal agent of death, nothing is made of this duality; it
generates no significance. There is no ironic juxtaposition of
his two roles, as there would be in *Women in Love;* we are not
maneuvred into adopting, simultaneously or nearly so, conflicting attitudes to corruption or decay.

The final paragraphs of the novel, which are commonly acknowledged to be unconvincing, bear upon my argument with
especial force. There is a demonstrable confusion of imagery in
these paragraphs, amounting in fact to a sort of trickery—but of
a kind that shows Lawrence feeling his way toward the richer
effects of *Women in Love.*

> She knew that the sordid people who crept hardscaled and separate
> on the face of the world's corruption were living still. . . . She saw in
> the rainbow the earth's new architecture, the old, brittle corruption
> of houses and factories swept away, the world built up in a living fab-
> ric of Truth, fitting to the over-arching heaven.

The hardness that Ursula discovers around her is both the hardness of death and a hardness that conceals new life. We are asked
to believe that the one kind of hardness can become or virtually *is*
the other, and on grounds that appear to be little more than verbal.
"The terrible corruption spreading over the face of the land" is
hard, dry, brittle; and equally hard, dry and brittle is the "horny
covering of disintegration," "the husk of an old fruition" in which
Ursula can observe "the swelling and the heaving contour of the
new germination." Lawrence insists on the completeness and
seeming finality of the corruption—it is "triumphant and un-
opposed"—and yet it is in the very extremity of the corruption that
consolation is discovered. If organisms have everywhere disin-
tegrated almost to dust, so much the better. The more dust-like,
the more easily "swept away"! Some such spurious logic would
seem to be implied, surely, in the collocation of "swept away,"

"brittle corruption" and "disintegration," and even if this were
not so, one's other objection would remain: the hardness of corruption ("corruption so pure that it is hard and brittle") cannot be
translated by mere verbal sleight-of-hand into the hardness of the
husk that encloses new life.

In any case, we are left with the impression that corruption
is merely *antithetical* to this new life—an impression that quite
fails to correspond with the fact that the novel has been moving
toward the discovery that corruption can also energize and renew.
The sequence in which this movement is most emphatic is that
concerned with Skrebensky's sinister African sensuality, where,
as we have seen, the language affirms both the menace of corruption and its life-giving potency. (The concept of corruption is
not invoked explicitly in the passage, but it is clearly within call;
the African night is at once hot and fluid, and there is a powerful
suggestion of over-abundant growth.) In the novel as a whole however, the movement in question, the tendency toward a simultaneous affirmation of corruption and vitality, is at least as much
promise as realization.

> Awful and threatening it was, dangerous to a degree, even whilst he
> gave himself to it. It was pure darkness, also. All the shameful things
> of the body revealed themselves to him now with a sort of sinister,
> tropical beauty. All the shameful natural and unnatural acts of sen-
> sual voluptuousness which he and the woman partook of together,
> created together, they had their heavy beauty and their delight.
> shame, what was it? It was part of extreme delight. It was that part of
> delight of which man is usually afraid. Why afraid? The secret, shame-
> ful things are most terribly beautiful.

There is not much horror in these tropics, obviously. "Sort of"
necessarily deprives "sinister" of some of its force, and the analogy
in any case is only a glancing one (by contrast one thinks of the
African sequence, later, and of that very real Negro "with his
loose, soft passion"). In short, while the beauty and the energizing
power of corruption (or something like corruption) are made
sufficiently real, the alternative possibilities of ugliness and nausea
tend to be distanced. And though this is a strategy that might appear to be locally justified, in the larger perspective it begins to
look suspect. For it is in keeping with the too-easy translation of
the reductive impulses into the constructive which I have already
commented on apropos of the conclusion of this episode, and to
that extent contributes significantly to the relative disorganization
of the novel in its latter phases.

David Cavitch

On Women in Love

Women in Love has a heterogeneous cast of characters that nearly equals the universality and contrivance of *Moby-Dick*. The social classes are all represented, from sordid working-class lovers up to the titled nobility of England and the Continent, though the most prominent characters are middle-class and semi-professional people and bohemian artists. The mixture of personal types and origins blends realistically in the novel's social focus that is chiefly the sophisticated world of "advanced" and "emancipated" personalities. A Jew, a Russian, an Arab servant, an Italian countess, a British baronet, a Fraulein, a French governess, a German sculptor—each minor figure contributes some detail to the atmosphere of universal depravity and psychological dissolution that pervades the fiction. The numerous references to other cultures also generalize the theme, for they carry overtones of the destruction that came to earlier societies at a peak of their development. During an outburst of fury by his former mistress, Birkin is smashed over the head with a paperweight while he sits reading Thucydides' account of the fall of Athens. Birkin repeatedly recalls the fate of Sodom when he reflects on the decadence of contemporary people. The Italian countess reads Turgenev's analysis of moral anarchism in nineteenth-century Russia in *Fathers and Sons*. With detail upon detail Lawrence reinforces his statement that civilizations compound and express the force of corruption within individual lives.

The analysis of individual consciousness, however, is the principal intent of the novel, and the sense that grave troubles infect us is established in the first chapter—though many critics have noted that the opening scene disarmingly suggests a Jane Austen comedy about the reassertion of good hearts and civil manners. Ursula and Gudrun, sitting in the window-bay of their parents' substantial house in Beldover, where Ursula recuperated at the end of *The Rainbow,* discuss love and the prospect of marriage; and like vain

From D. H. Lawrence and the New World *by David Cavitch. Copyright* ©*1969 by David Cavitch. Reprinted by permission of Oxford University Press, Inc.*

or superior young ladies in fiction of more than a century earlier they are afraid that all married men are bores and that married life will not sustain the sense of heightened significance, the romantic vividness, that they require in life. Ursula complains that marriage is more than likely to be "the end of experience," and Gudrun extends this despondent observation with a comment about the dreariness of even their present lives: "Don't you find, that things fail to materialize? *Nothing materializes!* Everything withers in the bud." It is true, just as one expects from this sketch of the opening, that both women meet men who rouse their profoundest love and that the true nature and desires of each character do materialize. But within this narrative development the tone of presentation is ominous, not expectant. The *bud,* in Gudrun's reference to life in general, blossoms into a *fleur du mal* or a "flower of dissolution," which is Lawrence's phrase for the corrupt soul; and the essential natures of most of the characters are so badly disfigured psychologically that catastrophe and death fulfill their hearts' real desires.

The cause of their misery is, as always in Lawrence's view, a sensual failure, a breakdown of the human will to live an individual life. Throughout *Women in Love,* Lawrence and his spokesman, Birkin, try to promulgate a new set of values to recover the will and the means to natural fulfillment. Birkin preaches the viability of conjugal love as a foundation for all other human values, and every effort is made in the novel to convince us that the center of man's experience must be, as Birkin tells Gerald, a "perfect union with a woman—sort of ultimate marriage—and there isn't anything else." Such a marriage would reach deeper into character than a relationship of conscious love, Birkin believes, and it alone can revive the "stark, unknown beings" that people fundamentally are. "What I want is a strange conjunction with you," he explains to Ursula in a confession of love that disappoints her expectations of more romantic language; "not meeting and mingling . . . —but an equilibrium, a pure balance of two single beings:—as the stars balance each other."

Birkin disavows the love-ideals that mask the violation of selves through "meeting and mingling," and "merging," and the clichéd patterns of being "in love." The principle of "balance" or *polarity* in love is fundamental to sensual vitality, he believes, for it preserves the inner, individual self intact. Though marriage offers the only opportunity for profound self-fulfillment, it paradoxically makes the severest attack upon one's separate identity. As an aid to maintaining "equilibrium," Birkin recommends another bond outside of marriage: an "eternal union with a man too: another kind of love." He looks to manly love as a necessary support to marriage and as a liberating extension of our unconscious life into a revivified civilization. Birkin achieves his "ultimate marriage" with Ursula, but lacking any enduring connection with another man he remains haunted by doom. At the end of the novel, as he sits over the body of Gerald who allowed himself to freeze to death in the mountains, Birkin feels devastated by the failure of their *Blutbruderschaft,* which would have given his friend strength to live if Gerald had held true to it. Weeping, he denounces the futile outcome of their friendship, and to the skeptical Ursula he insists that Gerald's acceptance of his offered love would have made a difference to them all. Birkin worries that neither mankind's self-destruction nor his own nagging "process of dissolution" can be arrested by the love in marriage only. But Ursula maintains a critical attitude in the concluding dialogue, and she condemns his interest in manly love as "an obstinacy, a theory, a perversity."

The end of the novel is filled with the air of tragic sorrow in Birkin's response to Gerald's death. His bitter lament indirectly eulogizes Gerald as the representative modern man, as he appears to most readers and critics—the ablest, fairest member of a society in which all men are doomed by their common limitation. Birkin's bitterness and grief alternate with his desperate conjecture that the total destruction of a man is not truly a reason for despair. He tries to console himself with his old opinion that man is expendable in the universe, and that a humanless world will "carry on the embodiment of creation" after mankind plunges into oblivion. But his recurring pronouncements upon man's insignificance are seen throughout the fiction as the misanthropy of self-loathing which afflicts him. At one point, Ursula mocks him for trying to believe "simply in the end of the world, and in grass." In his self-renewal through love for her, Birkin casts off his "sham spirituality," his death-eating," that Ursula excoriates in their lovers' quarrel. The reappearance of his outworn viewpoint emphasizes Birkin's pathetic sense of futility over Gerald's momentous death. *Women in Love* concludes with the dramatization of an irrevocable loss that is both personal and universal, for the whole of the novel mourns the imminent end of *man,* and no sophistry about life continuing without him remains equal to the emotion that is sustained in the last chapter.

W. W. Robson finds that in the tragic tone of the conclusion the tale asserts its own moral: that the kind of love which Birkin sought has proved illusory. But the novel fully dramatizes the triumph of his love with Ursula, a triumph of sensual will that has enabled them to break all their connections with society and with apparent success to "wander away from the world's somewhere, into our nowhere." The bitter defeat in Birkin's history is the failure of his ideal of manly love, which threatens to undermine all love and marriage. His desire for an "eternal union" with Gerald is not merely a stubborn theory, as Ursula dismisses it, nor is the theme separable from the novel's investigation of love between men and women. The friendship between Birkin and Gerald unifies the otherwise divided structure of the novel, for the romances of the two couples have one central source and development in their analysis of homoerotic desire. Gerald's suicide has an air of tragedy because the emotional focus of the book as a whole, including the interest of the author and the sequence of narrative events, makes Gerald seem the most admired sexual figure and the dominant erotic presence in the fiction. When his death shows that love between men is probably impossible, both Birkin and Lawrence respond with a grief far more desperate and moving than their sorrow over woman's love. The heartbreak over Gerald is unmatched in Lawrence's work except at the conclusion of *Sons and Lovers* when Lawrence suffers with Paul over the death of Mrs. Morel. The comparable intensity of feeling in these situations suggests their connection in the soul of the author, where all the fictional characters and events reveal Lawrence's unconscious. Birkin's quest for homoerotic love is a consequence of Paul's romance with his mother, and both experiences lead to the defeat of a forbidden, covert, supreme desire. The differences in subject and argument between the two works show how many complexities Lawrence was discovering in his experience of foredoomed love.

Lawrence was probably pursuing an actual homosexual romance in one or more of his friendships while writing *Women in Love*. Frieda refers vaguely to such a period in his life, and in *Kangaroo* Lawrence recounts the misery of such a relationship during his Cornwall years specifically.* But quite apart from his biographical suggestion, it is evident from a rejected Prologue to *Women in Love* that Lawrence at this time strongly felt that homoeroticism was the chief complication in all sexual experience. In the unpublished first chapter Lawrence gives a full report of Birkin's tormented homosexual desires and an account of the mutual erotic attraction between him and Gerald. The opening paragraphs re-

*This refers to Somers' friendship with John Thomas. There is no evidence to suggest a homosexual relationship between them. [*ed. note.*]

count their initial meeting in the Tyrol four years earlier, when each man instantly "knew the trembling nearness" of the other, and though they maintain reserve and neither one acknowledges it: "they knew they loved each other, that each would die for the other." During the four years before they meet again at the beginning of the novel's narrative action, Birkin suffers from his sexual ambivalence which he cannot accept morally. His desires, nevertheless, are fully conscious: men rouse his sexual passion, and he longs to possess the bodies of nameless strangers. He is intoxicated by the sexual beauty of two types of men:

> White-skinned, keen limbed men with eyes like blue-flashing ice and hair like crystals of winter sunshine, the northmen, inhuman as sharp-crying gulls, distinct like splinters of ice, like crystals, isolated, individual; and then the men with dark eyes that one can enter and plunge into, bathe in, as in a liquid darkness, dark-skinned, supple, night-smelling men, who are the living substance of the viscous, universal heavy darkness.

In this report of Birkin's homoerotic feelings, one immediately recognizes the sensations and the very words that in the novel are not Birkin's but Gudrun's responses to Gerald and to Loerke, who typify the two classes of sexually attractive men. Lawrence transferred to her the feelings that would have been Birkin's if his homosexuality had become explicitly the central issue in the fiction. Her distorted feelings of love—her pursuit of pain in sexual contact with brutal, relentless force—has no other origin or consonance in the novel. Gudrun is physically and mentally glamorous, full of young beauty, strength, awareness, and pride. Yet she is damned to pursue extreme psychological and sexual sensations in which she anticipates her doom. The paradox—plausible as it could be among the complexities of an actual life—is never made comprehensible in the fiction. The only explanation for her character is that Lawrence chose to make her the vehicle of feelings that he originally understood to be homoerotic, and that her responses give evidence of Lawrence's shame and anxiety over such desires.

It is possible that Lawrence was trying to minimize or disguise his views about homosexuality, especially since the suppression of *The Rainbow* had just shown him that the treatment of sex in fiction could not be freely outspoken. Birkin's latent homosexuality remains prominent through implication even without the Prologue to clarify his psychology, and Gerald's troubled sexual response to Birkin appears clearly in the episodes that dramatize his resistance to their *Blutbruderschaft.* But the important effect of transferring Birkin's sensations onto Gudrun is that the change generalizes Lawrence's views. He shifts the atmosphere of perversion on to heterosexual relations, alleging them to be hopelessly complicated by homosexual ambivalence. Gerald and Gudrun anticipate the fulfillment of their romance in an aura of revulsion, hysteria, and disaster. The sado-masochism of their affair is fully described, but its causes remain half hidden in Lawrence's implication that both Gerald and Gudrun—even more then Birkin—need "another kind of love."

In the opening chapter Gudrun instantly recognizes that Gerald is her destined lover, because of his air of invulnerable sexual mastery. She thrills with anticipation of some extreme conflict between them, and throughout the first half of the novel she reels with excitement at every meeting with Gerald. Her passion exalts her fear of violence in masculine sexuality, which she hopes to master by her attitude of exquisite subjection. Gerald's response to her, however, develops much slower and more deviously; his attraction to Gudrun is not a direct response to her but a displacement of feelings roused in him by other circumstances.

The doom that pervades Gerald's life is not his fear of heterosexual love but his rejection of love between men. His "process of dissolution" that ends in suicide begins with his accidental killing of his brother, for that act comes to symbolize his denial of any life-tie among men. He is fundamentally a "murderer," as Lawrence warns us in the second chapter, and all of his energies serve to destroy life for him and for others. After his definitive childhood "accident" Gerald pursues his own death through violent masculine exploits as a soldier, explorer, and sportsman. He is repeatedly placed amidst water and snow as a swimmer or skier, and the cold, aqueous substances which are his special element in the novel consistently suggest Gerald's attraction to death. In his social role, Gerald projects his own despair of life onto a whole class of society. As a leading industrialist, he modernizes the coal-mining industry and settles the series of strikes and labor riots at the Crich family's mines. With intuitive sympathy for the miners' sense of degradation by technological changes, Gerald leads the workers to revere mechanical productiveness itself because he senses that worship of the machine exalts their inhuman, repetitive actions. After a period of violent resistance to modernization, the men—like Gerald's mistress—find a perverse satisfaction in

abandoning themselves to his power. The mining operation as re-organized by Gerald into an efficient industry expresses the common man's despair and rejection of spontaneous, warm life.
In Birkin as in others, Gerald rouses an anticipation of new knowledge and new activity. Gerald desires but hesitates to accept the attachment of manly love that Birkin would freely welcome as an adjunct to marriage. Birkin recognizes that Gerald's resistance is upheld by a defining, fixed principle of his character that prevents any widening of his experience:

> This strange sense of fatality in Gerald, as if he were limited to one form of existence, one knowledge, one activity, a sort of fatal half-ness, which to himself seemed wholeness, always overcame Birkin after thier moments of passionate approach, and filled him with a sort of contempt, or boredoms. I was the insistence on the limitation which so bored Birkin in Gerald.

After Birkin's illness occasions a crisis of erotic feelings in their friendship, Gerald finds himself bored with all his usual satisfactions—work, sexual adventures, hashish, or travel. He recovers new spirit only when Birkin visits him one night and the two men abandon themselves to frenzied physical contact by wrestling. Birkin tries to explain to him that their intimacy and physical attraction are perfectly wholesome: "'We are mentally, spiritually intimate, therefore we should be more or less physically intimate too—it is more whole.'" Though Gerald agrees to Birkin's happy rational conclusion, he remains troubled and confused by the power of his feeling for a man. At the end of the chapter, "Gladitorial," Gerald haltingly confesses that he does not expect love for a woman to equal his genuine love for Birkin. After "a long pause," Birkin answers cautiously and vaguely in an effort to encourage his friend: "'Life has all kinds of things,' said Birkin. 'There isn't only one road.'" But the desperate tone of Gerald's response indicates his distress over pursuing any other than the usual satisfactions. Frightened by the appeal of a "blood-brotherhood," he can conceive of his fulfillment only as ominous and final:

> "Yes, I believe that too. I believe it. And mind you, I don't care how it is with me—I don't care how it is—so long as I don't feel—" he paused, and a blank, barren look passed over his face, to express his feeling—"so long as I feel I've *lived*, somehow—and I don't care how it is—but I want to feel that—"

Precisely at this halfway point in the narrative, Gerald's casual attraction to Gudrun turns into a consuming passion that supersedes any further development of love between him and Birkin. Gerald surprises himself and astonishes the elated Gudrun by declaring his love for her. Gudrun, who looks on Gerald with rapacious expectation of sinister pleasures, captures all the force of Gerald's conflicting needs. She offers to satisfy his pent-up desire for a sexual experience that transgresses his psychological limits, and she also preserves his belief in his glamorous masculinity. Gudrun holds Gerald entranced with desire for a woman, while he experiences with her the "licentiousness"—the sexual extremism and barbaric feelings—that would characterize his guilt-ridden participation in a homosexual act. He turns to her in a passion of flight from the alternative that Birkin's love presents.

The circumstances of Gerald's first sexual intercourse with Gudrun illustrate that his desire for her signifies his psychological disintegration. The chapter "Death and Love" deals chiefly with Gerald's misery at home during the last days of the elder Crich, who as a macabre and pathetic death's-head figure has dominated the entire household throughout his long illness. In theme and feeling, the chapter centers in the unendurable strain of a protracted crisis, which Lawrence establishes in the opening sentences: "Thomas Crich died slowly, terribly slowly. It seemed impossible to everybody that the thread of life could be drawn out so thin, and yet not break." Thomas Crich's personal *will*—the fixed, rational purposiveness of his character—finally crumbles, and the death of the elder Crich illustrates the defeat of the principle by which Gerald attempts to dominate life. The fatal limitation that Birkin recognized in him was visibly broken down; but with full understanding of the tragedy in the psychological event, Lawrence shows that the breakdown of an evil principle in Gerald is an emotional degeneration, not a psychic triumph for him. In deep suffering, Gerald visits his father's fresh grave on a rainy night, and then desperately plunges toward the Brangwen house, where surreptitiously and dripping with clay he enters Gudrun's bedroom. Mutely demanding sexual consummation, Gerald empties himself of anxieties during a love-scene that is dominated by images of his infantile dependency. His turning to Gudrun in this context signifies a regressive response to the crisis of "invisible physical life" brought on by his father's dying. Unnerved, he settles himself through sexual exhaustion with Gudrun, and "he found in her an infinite relief."

The death of Thomas Crich occurs when Gerald is at a peak of disturbed vacillation over Birkin's love. The narrative structure coalesces Gerald's responses to these parallel mysteries of love and death, and in one definitive action Gerald evades both his crises.

His reaction is a narcissistic exploitation of Gudrun: "Like a child
at the breast, he cleaved intensely to her, and she could not put
him away." Broken by the knowledge of death and by a sexual
ambivalence that he cannot accept, Gerald's soul falls into a
"process of dissolution." In the remaining months of his life he
pursues the sensation of self-destruction in his affair with Gudrun,
demanding specifically the explosive force of tortured orgasm,
while Gudrun easily dominates him by offering herself only to his
frenzies of abuse. He explains to Birkin that Gudrun is his supreme
experience, and his expression reveals that in loving Gudrun he
seeks only the final obliteration of consciousness:

> "There's something final about this. And Gudrun seems like the
> end, to me. I don't know—but she seems so soft, her skin like silk,
> her arms heavy and soft. And it withers my consciousness, somehow,
> it burns the pith of my mind." He went on a few paces, staring ahead,
> his eyes fixed, looking like a mask used in ghastly religions of the
> barbarians. "It blasts your soul's eye," he said, "and leaves you sight-
> less. Yet you *want* to be sightless, you *want* to be blasted, you don't
> want it any different."
> He was speaking as if in a trance, verbal and blank. Then sud-
> denly he braced himself up with a kind of rhapsody, and looked at
> Birkin with vindictive, cowed eyes, saying:
> "Do you know what it is to suffer when you are with a woman?
> She's so beautiful, so perfect, you find her *so good,* it tears you like a
> silk, and every stroke and bit cuts hot—ha, that perfection, when you
> blast yourself, you blast youself! And then—" he stopped on the snow
> and suddenly opened his clenched hands—"it's nothing—your brain
> might have gone charred as rags—and—" he looked round into the air
> with a queer histrionic movement—"it's blasting—you understand
> what I mean—it is a great experience, something final—and then—
> you're shrivelled as if struck by electricity." He walked on in silence.
> It seemed like bragging, but like a man in extremity bragging truth-
> fully.
> "Of course," he resumed, "I wouldn't *not* have had it! It's a com-
> plete experience. And she's a wonderful woman. But—how I hate her
> somewhere! It's curious—"
> Birkin looked at him, at his strange, scarcely conscious face.
> Gerald seemed blank before his own words.
> "But you've had enough now?" said Birkin. "You have had your
> experience. Why work on an old wound?"
> "Oh," said Gerald, "I don't know. It's not finished—"

The finish occurs when Gerald in an unendurable rage against
Gudrun is overcome by nausea and revulsion for all of life. He

drops her in the snow, half-strangled, and he turns away to meet his death by freezing on the mountain peaks. The catastrophe takes place amidst the symbolic landscape of the Tyrol, where Lawrence in the Prologue had originally begun the romance between Gerald and Birkin. The extended description of the place itself is one of Lawrence's finest achievements in the novel, for the crystalline and massive landscape, which is breathtakingly vivid, comes to be emotionally abhorrent as it reveals its symbolic meaning. The Alpine setting is the culmination of Lawrence's identifications between Gerald's condition of rigidly limited consciousness and all *cold* substances. The mountain is also the geographical image of the "slope of death" which Birkin has pictured as the present footing of the northern European soul in its last stage of dissolution. The kinesthetic force of the landscape mirrors the crushing antagonism that lies scarcely below the surface of heterosexual love between Gerald and Gudrun. In the sequence of composition that reveals Lawrence's discoveries and developing judgments about his subject, the place of budding love between man and man becomes the final setting that commemorates like a tombstone man's demented will to crush the life out of himself. In this, as in every way, the novel implies that the bitterness of the heterosexual affair and Gerald's tragic death are the consequences of man's fear to love his friend.

The story of Birkin, who is the central figure in the novel, is intended to illustrate the triumph of the psychically liberated man who learns to acknowledge his homoerotic feelings and to value them as part of his full, spontaneous sensual nature. Birkin's moods of despair and petulance early in the narrative are signs of a crippled emotional state, in which for years he has prolonged an ambiguous affair with Hermione. Even without the Prologue's explanation one sees that Birkin's life is complicated by a fear of women and a sensual attraction to men. Roused to new love in his relationship with Ursula, he slowly manages to erase his image of her as a Magna Mater full of Woman's greed to possess and dismember her sexual victim. Birkin's progress toward a sane response to Ursula is measured chiefly by their extended discussions about love and by their mercurial quarrels that displace his fears and allow the lovers to express trust and tenderness. But along with this love story, the narrative traces the simultaneous growth of Birkin's attraction to Gerald. Birkin more ardently and openly seeks Gerald's love as his romance with Ursula proves successful and vivifying for him. Lawrence hoped to show through Birkin that the free, unified man will express his sensual affections, his un-

conscious feelings, in every relationship with things and persons—
not just with the opposite sex. Lawrence relived Birkin of the
guilty feelings that in the Prologue complicated his desires in
order to make him into a test-case of the exemplary, "new world"
man. When Gerald perversely dies, however, neither Birkin nor
Lawrence can overcome the feeling that the ideal of manly love
has resulted in catastrophe—and the novel concludes with this
misgiving and lament.

The failure of the homoerotic ideal in *Women in Love* left
Lawrence's ambivalence toward women more acute than before.
Disposed to identify with his female characters as the vessels of
sensual life in *Sons and Lovers* and *The Rainbow,* he was at the
same time hypersensitive to any distortions of masculine identity,
and he held women responsible for the possessive love that warps
an individual's natural integrity. In *Women in Love* Lawrence
more analytically explores the ambiguities that account for love's
strange facts. His characterization of Birkin shows that Birkin's
image of the devouring female expresses, in part, his fascinated
dread of being assaulted as a female by a dismembering, "murder-
ing" male. In his corrective effort to love both woman and man,
Birkin's homosexual fantasy very nearly comes true. He is not
assaulted by Gerald, but it seems that Gerald averts that fate only
because he is psychologically constrained to destroy himself
rather than murder or "blast" his friend. Lawrence's own anxiety
over the male eros, which sets the tragic tone of the catastrophe,
leads him to undermine his analysis throughout the book by
dramatizing the fantasy explanation that woman destroys all
manliness. This charge against the devouring female, though dis-
proved by Ursula, is laid against Gudrun, whose genesis as Birkin's
persona remains evident in the novel. Birkin's failure to heal himself reinforces the emotional truth of Gudrun the man-as-woman,
the sexually defensive destroyer of natural life. The novel is true to
the author's feelings, but it betrayingly confirms his fears; and con-
sequently, this novel is followed by Lawrence's increasingly hostile
representations of women through his subsequent works, until he
desperately extricated himself from active sexuality altogether.*

* In "What Happened to D. H. Lawrence's *Goats and Compasses?*", *The D. H.
Lawrence Review* (Fall, 1971, 280–286), George Zytaruk argues convincingly that
the suppressed "Prologue" to *Women in Love (Phoenix II)* was intended as an intro-
ductory chapter to a projected novel, *Goats and Compasses,* which Cecil Gray,
who apparently saw the work, described as "a bombastic, pseudo-mystical, psycho-
philosophical treatise dealing largely with homosexuality." It may have been an
early, unfinished version of *Women in Love.*

Yudhishtar
The Changing Scene:
Aaron's Rod

In *Aaron's Rod,* as in *The Lost Girl,* the story opens in the English Midlands and then moves on to Italy—though the significance of the change in scene in the two novels cannot be said to be the same. *Aaron's Rod,* in fact, continues Lawrence's "life and thought adventure" at the point where *Women in Love* had left it, and further explores the theme of man-woman relationship, bringing out its limitations and inadequacies, and defining at length man's need for coming into possession of his own soul, for "his isolate self-responsibility." It is this central theme which unites many of the apparently unrelated episodes in the novel. Jim's harangues on love, as well as Lilly's on his relationship with Tanny—no less than Aaron's own experiences with Josephine Ford and the Marchesa del Torre—serve in their different ways to clarify Aaron's feeling of dissatisfaction arising out of the kind of relationship he has had with his wife. Birkin at the end of *Women in Love* leaves Ursula puzzled as to why, having her, he should still want an additional relationship with a man, too. *Aaron's Rod,* elaborating the theme, explains through an imaginatively conceived situation the need for man-to-man relationship, and goes on to experiment with one of the possible forms that such a relationship could assume.

Love, Lawrence believed, is only a traveling, not a goal; it is a process, not an end. There is no fulfilment in love itself, even though it can and should lead to "the fulfilment of single aloneness," to the "central fullness of self-possession." The central fulfilment for a man is that he should possess his own soul within him, "deep and alone." This deep, rich aloneness is reached and perfected through love, and only through love: but love, nevertheless, remains only a means to an end. "One has to learn," Lawrence says in a letter, "that love is a secondary thing in life. The first thing is to be a free, proud, single being by oneself: to be oneself free, to let the other be free: to force nothing and not to be forced oneself into anything. . . . Love isn't all that important: one's own

From Conflict in the Novels of D. H. Lawrence *by Yudhishtar. Oliver and Boyd, Ltd., 1969. Reprinted by permission.*

free soul is first." In marriage a man has his consummation and
his being: but the final consummation for him lies beyond marriage. Having deeply fulfilled himself in marriage, he should not
come to rest, but must undertake the responsibility for the next
step into the future by participating in some passionate, purposive
activity. Acting in his role as a "creator, mover, maker" man acts
in unison with other men in an "eternal" and "sacred relationship
of comrades"—which is the final progression from marriage:

> Let there be again the old passion of deathless friendship be-
> tween man and man. Humanity can never advance into the new re-
> gions of unexplored futurity otherwise. . . . Friendship should be a
> rare, choice, immortal thing, sacred and inviolable as marriage. Mar-
> riage and deathless friendship, both should be inviolable and sacred:
> two great creative passions, separate, apart, but complementary:
> the one pivotal, the other adventurous: the one, marriage, the centre
> of human life; and the other, the leap ahead.

One requisite for the establishment of a new, spontaneous relationship between men, it would appear, is that they should have a new
attitude toward one another—an attitude based on "a new re-
verence for their heroes" and "a new regard for their comrades."
Lawrence's views about "heroes" among men were to undergo a
change in the course of time, but when he wrote *Aaron's Rod* he
was still playing with the idea—though, as we shall see, not without a certain amount of scepticism.

With these views of Lawrence in mind we can now turn to
Aaron's Rod to consider the extent to which they can be said to
be embodied in the novel itself. There is, it would at once be apparent to any reader, only some general talk about "purposive
activity" in the book, the action of the novel containing little to
suggest this. (The explanation for this, however, might be that
Aaron has yet to attain "the stillness and sweet possession of [his]
own soul"; and it is only toward the end of the novel that he begins to do so.) Also, the novel ends on a very ambiguous note about
what the nature of Aaron's relationship with Lilly is going to be.
But otherwise the development of the novel follows, I think, the
general conception which I have tried to outline above.

Aaron Sisson, when the book opens just after the end of the
war, is still living with his family. He has been married twelve
years, and his relations with his wife are now coming to a crisis,
even though he is not consciously aware of it. The "sickness of
the unrecognised and incomprehensible strain" between him and
his wife has not only set him apart from her, but also cut him off

from his surroundings. The "curious and deadly opposition" between their two wills causes in Aaron a "nauseating ache" and a hostile tension which extends to include his relation with the rest of his "circumambient universe." He finds the "cosy brightness" of his home "unspeakably familiar" and unbearably monotonous: "The acute familiarity of this house, which had been built for his marriage twelve years ago, the changeless pleasantness of it all seemed unthinkable." For a time he has tried, and partially succeeded, in forgetting the deep feeling of antagonism toward his surroundings. "A woman and whisky, these were usually a remedy—and music." But now they have begun to fail him. He still wants to let himself go, to "feel rosy and loving and all that": but the hard opposing core in him—"this strained, unacknowledged opposition to his surroundings"—sits deep established in him like an obstinate black dog which growls and shows its teeth at the very thought of any connections. His aloofness and "dead-level indifference" to his surroundings is repeatedly stressed—until, about half-way through the novel, his soul begins to open up to the magic of life again while he is traveling in Italy. For the present he finds that his contact even with the landlady of the Royal Oak—in the "great fierce warmth" of whose presence he has so loved to luxuriate for some time past—is distasteful to him. Her very lustfulness, which had so pricked his senses once, now leaves him cold, even deadly antagonistic to her. The thought of his wife leaves him even whiter and colder, set in a more intense obstinacy. He has turned away from the possessive love and goodwill of his wife, only to encounter "righteous bullying" in all those he comes across. His unfaithfulness to his wife has only succeeded in making her will, like his own, strong and unrelaxing, so that there has come to exist a state of deadlock between them. Then, suddenly, Aaron leaves his wife and children and goes away. Why? Why does he go away like that? The question is asked several times in the book itself, and many critics have asked it since. It is, indeed, the crucial question in the novel, and the reader has a legitimate right to ask for an explanation. Does the book provide us with an answer?

Eliseo Vivas strongly condemns the book for its failure to elucidate the grounds on which Aaron, without any explanation or warning, decides to leave his family. "What justifies the action?" he asks, adding that he, as a critic, is asking for an aesthetic justification, not demanding a moral justification for "an unmitigatedly caddish act, a justification that will satisfy my notions of the decent treatment a man owes his family and himself." The terms in

which the case is put leads one to doubt if Vivas was really looking
for an "aesthetic" justification. It is probably true that neither
Aaron nor Lawrence has any explanation to offer which would
satisfy Mr. Vivas's "notions of decent treatment": but if all he
wanted was "a rendering, in whatever way the author chooses
to give it, of that which gives Aaron's action its intelligibility in
the story," then it is difficult to understand why he should have
failed to see that in one way the entire book is little more than an
attempt to do just that.

Aaron's marriage to Lottie, we are told, turns almost at once
into a relationship of conflict. It is not that they do not love each
other. Aaron has loved his wife and has "never loved any other
woman"; he has been a passionate lover, keeping back from her
"nothing, no experience, no degree of intimacy." Lottie, too, has
been passionately in love with him, has, indeed, "loved him to
madness." But this love soon turns into "a kind of combat." Both
of them have been brought up to consider themselves the first in
whatever company of relationship they find themselves. Besides,
Lottie has—not unexpectedly, though not quite consciously—
imbibed the formulated and professed belief of the whole white
world in "the life-centrality of woman." For this no blame is put
on her, as "this great and ignominious dogma of the sacred priority
of women" is shared not only by all other women but also by
practically all men. The whole world around her thinks of Woman
as the life-bearer, the life source, the center of creation—whereas
man is considered a mere adjunct. "She, as woman, and particularly as mother, was the first great source of life and being, and
also of culture. The man was but the instrument and the finisher.
She was the source and the substance." Aaron himself, on one
level, subscribes to this *"idee fixe* of today" that he should yield
himself, give himself away to his woman in order to achieve the
final consummation. In his "open mind" he has the ready-made
and banal idea of himself as a "really quite nice individual," and
from this comes his homage rendering love and worship of his
wife. For some time even Lottie is taken in by this manifest love.
But "though you can deceive the conscious mind, you can never
deceive the deep unconscious instinct." So she finds herself despising him in "her terrible paroxysms of hatred for him." She
cannot understand why she feels so dazed and maddened: for a
long time she does not realize that in spite of all the wonder and
miracle of their "heaven-rending passion" Aaron has been with-
holding the central core of himself, never giving himself to her.

"He cheated and made play with her tremendous passional soul, her sacred sex passion, most sacred of all things for a woman. All the time, some central part of him stood apart from her, aside, looking on." Aaron himself is not conscious of what is going on in his "passional soul" beneath his "conscious mask." But in him, we are informed by the narrator, is planted another seed. "Born in him was a spirit which could not worship woman: no, and would not. Could not and would not. It was not in him." Lottie, however, feels instinctively sure that her man must yield to her "so that she could envelop him, yielding, in her all-benificent love. She was quite sure her love was all benificent. Of this no shadow of doubt." Her profound impulse and instinct, developed in her by the age she lives in, tell her that to be perfectly enveloped in her benificent love is the highest her man can ever know or reach. But as time goes by she comes to realize that she can never fully possess him, and then she is filled with hate for him. . . .

Lottie, we are told, remains a good wife and mother, fulfilling all her duties. But of one thing she is dead certain: that in the conflict with her husband she must never yield, must never capitulate, or abandon her divine responsibility as woman. "*He* must yield. That was written in eternal letters, on the iron tablet of her will. *He* must yield. She the woman, the mother of his children, how should she ever think to yield? It was unthinkable. He, the man, the weak, the false, the treacherous, the half-hearted, it was he who must yield."

In order to escape his wife's terrible will—which, like a "flat cold snake coiled round his soul," is squeezing him to death— Aaron first takes to leaving her alone as much as possible, then is unfaithful to her. Lottie is "more than maddened": but he begins to be quite indifferent to her. Then she, too, learns to be indifferent to the fascination he exerts over her, and fights him with her powerful will "which presses and presses and cannot relax." Two wills are now wound tense and fixed. "She became the same as he. Even in her moments of most passionate desire for him, the cold and snake-like tension of her will never relaxed, and the cold, snake-like eye of her intention never closed." The conflict, however, does not take place on a conscious level, and "neither of them understood what was happening." There is, nevertheless, a deadlock between them, with neither of the two wills relaxing. At the point where the novel opens Aaron has just come to the realization that at this "terrible passive game of fixed tension" Lottie would beat him.

Her fixed female soul, her wound-up female will would solidify into stone—whereas his must break. In him something must break. It was a cold and fatal deadlock, profitless. A life-automatism of fixed tension that suddenly, in him, did break. His will flew loose in a recoil: a recoil away from her. He left her, as inevitably as a broken spring flies from its hold.

Aaron is not yet fully conscious why he has left his wife. Lottie has no idea, either, why he has deserted her. She is aware that in his relationship with her he "kept himself back, always kept himself back, couldn't give himself:" but she does not connect this with Aaron's going away. She rather attributes his leaving her "with all the burden" to his being "selfish through and through;" later, she tells him that he ran away because he was "too weak," "unnatural and evil," "unmanly and cowardly." Actually, she is completely puzzled by his conduct and can think of no convincing explanation for it. Aaron himself can only feel the unrelaxing tension within him, and goes away hating "the hard, inviolable heart that stuck unchanging in his own breast." When he is asked by Josephine Ford why he had left his wife, he has "no particular reason" to offer.[1] On her insistence that he could not have left his wife and little girls for no reason at all, he still says:

> "Yes, I did. For no reason—except I wanted to have a bit of free room round me—to loose myself."
> "You mean you wanted love?" flashed Josephine, thinking he said *lose.*
> "No, I wanted fresh air. I don't know what I wanted. Why should I know?"
> "But we must know: especially when other people are going to suffer so," said she.
> "Ah well! A breath of fresh air, by myself. I felt forced to love. I feel if I go back home now, I shall be *forced*—forced to love—or care—or something."
> "Perhaps you wanted more than your wife could give you," she said.
> "Perhaps less. She's made up her mind she loves me, and she's not going to let me off."

---

[1] In a later conversation with Sir William Frank at Novara, Aaron compares his abandoning his wife and children to a "natural event," as undeniable as birth or death. "It wasn't a question of reasons," he says, "It was a question of her and me and what must be." Aaron, though quite certain of the inevitability of his action, does not yet "know"—and therefore cannot explain—what he feels in his "passional soul."

"Did you never love her?" said Josephine.

"Oh yes. I shall never love anybody else. But I'm damned if I want to go on being a lover, to her or to anybody. That's the top and bottom of it. I don't want to *care,* when care isn't in me. And I'm not going to be forced to it."

Aaron's assertion that he is not going to care when care is not in him is—though he himself is not yet clear about its implications—an instinctive rejection on his part of "duty" and "responsibility" in terms of social morality, and an acceptance of a deeper moral responsibility to himself. He is still—we are told—attached to his family, and has arranged for sufficient money to be paid over to his wife, having "reserved only a small amount for himself:" but he is not prepared to yield the mastery of his own soul and conscience and actions to anyone else. When, overcome by qualms concerning his abandoned family, he returns home after almost a year's absence, he is torn by conflicting emotions. "The place, the home, at once fascinated him and revolted him." He foresees a "violent emotional reconciliation" with his wife, and is filled with a "violent conflict of tenderness:" but when he actually meets her and hears her voice which is "full of hate," he is again overcome by the old "sickness of the unrecognised and incomprehensible strain between him and her." She challenges him to tell her what he has against her: "Tell me! Tell me what I've done." But "telling isn't so easy—especially when the trouble goes too deep for conscious comprehension. He couldn't *tell* what he had against her. And he had not the slightest intention of doing what she would have liked him to do, starting to pile up detailed grievances. He knew the detailed grievances were nothing in themselves." Even when Lottie is ready for a reconciliation and wistfully appeals to him to confess that he has been wrong to her, he cannot do it because beneath her pleading he can feel "the iron of her heart." . . .

Both Aaron and Lottie are too rigid in their attitudes for the conflict between them to find any resolution. Aaron, therefore, resolves on "life single, not life double." For the time being, he decides, his need is to be alone, to be himself: "Let there be clean and pure division first, perfected singleness. That is the only way to final, living unison: through sheer, finished singleness."

Aaron returns to London; then finding that the town "got on his nerves," determines to clear out. Knowing that Lilly has gone to Italy, he decides to follow him there. It is in Italy, at Novara, that one Sunday evening Aaron, for the first time, becomes vaguely conscious of "the root cause of his strife with Lottie." He knows that in the kind of deadlock that exists between them neither of the two can be wholly at fault and that he himself is partly to blame. "Having a detached and logical soul, he never let himself forget this truth." But whereas he was puzzled before, not knowing why there was so much conflict in his relations with his wife, now—even if he can see no solution—it is at least a defined situation:

> He realised that he had never intended to yield himself fully to her or to anything: that he did not intend ever to yield himself up entirely to her or to anything: that his very being pivoted on the fact of his isolate self-responsibility, aloneness. His intrinsic and central aloneness was the very centre of his being. Break it, and he broke his being. Break this central aloneness, and he broke everything. It was the great temptation, to yield himself: and it was the final sacrilege. Anyhow, it was something which, from his profoundest soul, he did not intend to do. By the innermost isolation and singleness of his own soul he would abide though the skies fell on top of one another, and seven heavens collapsed.

This realization comes to Aaron not as so many words or ideas; with him it is more a case of silent, "wordless comprehension." But in his own "powerful but subconscious" fashion Aaron becomes aware that he had never wanted, and does not want, to surrender himself utterly to either his wife or anybody else.

> The last extreme of self-abandon in love was for him an act of false behaviour. His own nature inside him fated him not to take this last false step, over the edge of the abyss of selflessness. Even if he wanted to, he could not. . . . For, according to all the current prejudice and impulse in one direction, he too had believed that the final achievement, the consummation of human life, was this flinging oneself over the precipice, down the bottomless pit of love. Now he realised that love, even in its intensest, was only an attribute of the human soul: one of its incomprehensible gestures. And to fling down the whole soul in one gesture of finality in love was as much a criminal suicide as to jump off a church-tower or a mountain-peak. Let a man give himself as much as he liked in love, to seven thousand extremities, he must never give himself *away*. The more generous and the more passionate a soul, the more it *gives* itself. But the more absolute remains the law, that it shall never give itself away. Give thyself, but give thyself not away.

This "splendid love-way" requires that both man and woman should maintain their separate identity in the relationship of love. Aaron has at last come to accept the necessity of being by himself —recognizing that his state of loneliness is in itself a fulfilment in so far as it marks the completion of a great stage in the process of love. The attainment of singleness or aloneness, however, is only a preparation for fuller and more vital relationships in the next stage. Aaron has so far been only breaking loose from one connection after another, snapping all old ties which had bound him to the people he has loved or liked. In a way he knows that he is thus "fulfilling his own inward destiny:" but he also feels apprehensive at where it is leading him. "Why break every tie?" he asks himself, "In God's name, why? What was there instead?" And the answer he gets is: nothingness. "There was just himself and blank nothingness." He realizes that for the time being he is not moving *toward* anything, only moving away from everything. He is not seeking for love, or for any kind of unison or communion. "Only let him *not* run into any sort of embrace with anything or anybody—this was what he asked. Let no new connection be made between himself and anything on earth. Let all old connections break. This was his craving." But sooner or later he must fall back into relationship—for cut off from all vital contacts he can only arrive at "blank nothingness." His very individuality, his "singleness" itself, is dependent on relationship. He, of course, cannot force himself into any living relationship, but must wait till some connection naturally forms itself without any interference by him. Aaron's isolation from his wife and children had, in turn, led to his alienation from his surroundings. Now, in the reversal of the process, he succeeds first in establishing a rapport with the natural surroundings before he can enter into any meaningful human relationship.

Considerable prominence is given in the novel to the subject of Aaron's loss of contact with his "circumambient universe;" and it is, significantly, in Italy that he begins to get in touch with it again. The beautiful view he has on his very first morning in Novara—the winding river, the clear, clean air, the massive snow-streaked mountains—all this makes the universe live for him again for a time. The Alps seem to him like "tigers prowling between the north and the south;" the wind coming from the snow is like "the icy whiskers of a tiger:" Aaron's "old sleepy English nature" is startled in its sleep. But he is not yet ready to come awake, not wanting to face the responsibility of the new life rising in him:

To open his darkest eyes and wake up to a new responsibility.
Wake up and enter on the responsibility of a new self in himself.
Ach, the horror of responsibility! He had all his life slept and shelved
the burden. And he wanted to go on sleeping. . . . He felt some finger
prodding, prodding, prodding him awake out of the sleep of pathos
and tragedy and spasmodic passion, and he wriggled unwilling, oh
most unwilling to undertake the new business.

Aaron can sense a new life-quality everywhere around him and
is aware of the dynamically different values of life in the country
he has come to. But his mind and soul are not fully opened up to
this new "spontaneous life-dynamic." Some days later, traveling
by rail from Milan to Florence on a "lovely, lovely day of early
autumn," he is again struck by the bigness and the exposed beauty
of the great plain of Lombardy. There seems to him a kind of bold-
ness and openness in the landscape which impresses and fascinates
him. Looking at his companions in the third-class carriage, he finds
the same quality of indifference and exposed gesture in them, too.

It is, finally, in Florence—in the Piazza della Signoria with
its "clownish Bandinellis" and the Michaelangelo's David—that
Aaron feels he has come to "one of the world's living centres,"
and feels a new self, a new life-surge rising inside himself. "Florence seemed to start a new man in him."

As "a new man" Aaron not only feels free to get in touch with
other human beings, but also succeeds, with the help of his flute,
in performing the "little miracle" of awakening a new woman in
the Marchesa del Torre. For a long time he had been gripped inside himself, hard and unyielding, his desire for women fast with-
held. "All his deep, desirous blood had been locked, he had wanted
nobody, and nothing. And it had been hard to live, so. Without
desire, without any movement of passionate love, only gripped
back in recoil! That was an experience to endure." Now his desire
comes back, strong and fierce. He feels his turn has at last come,
that Aaron's rod is going to blossom again: "The phoenix had
risen in fire again, out of the ashes." The Marchesa, who had been
for years shut in the "dank and beastly dungeon of feelings and
moral necessity," also feels free to establish a connection with
Aaron "outside the horrible, stinking human castle of life." But
for Aaron this relationship can be a success only if it proves to be
radically different in nature from his earlier relations with women
and leaves his intrinsic, inviolable self alone. It is not for nothing
that he had left his wife, and had found that his experience with
Josephine Ford nearly killed him, because he had been forced to
"give in." As it turns out, his relation with the Marchesa brings

to him, at the very start, an awareness of the conflict within him. Realizing that he is "sinking towards her," Aaron is terrified at the prospect of his being absorbed by her, and yet he also *wants* to sink toward her:

> The flesh and blood of him simply melted out, in desire towards her. Cost what may, he must come to her. And yet he knew at the same time that, cost what may, he must keep the power to recover himself from her. He must have his cake and eat it.

But he cannot both eat his cake and have it. The Marchesa, we gather from her husband's reflections on Eve, is the woman who merely takes a man to use him, to make of him that which will serve her desire. "She may love me," he says, "she may be soft and kind to me, she may give her life for me. But why? Only because I am *hers.* I am that thing which does her most intimate service." It does not take Aaron long to discover that the Marchesa completely ignores him as an individual and uses him "as a mere magic implement;" that unless she herself wills it, his "male power"—of which he is so proud—can cast no spell on her. She rather seems, by withstanding him, to throw "cold water over his phoenix newly risen from the ashes of its nest in flames." Yet his will is fixed on possessing her "whole soft white body . . . in its entirety, its fulness." That he finds this "soft white body" also "deadly in power" should come as no surprise. Like Skrebensky's desire for Ursula in *The Rainbow,* his passion for the Marchesa is "just unalloyed desire, and nothing else." There is no personal intimacy or tenderness in the relationship: it is all sheer destructive sensuality. No wonder then that "his desire and himself likewise [break] disastrously under the proving." Seeing that Aaron had found his fuller relationship (of passion as well as tenderness) with Lottie unsatisfactory because it violated his "intrinsic and central aloneness," it was inevitable that his self-seeking relationship with the Marchesa should leave him with the feeling that "it simply blasted his own central life." . . .

Aaron's relation with the Marchesa both serves to clarify the nature of conflict in his relationship with Lottie and to bring to him a renewed and intensified awareness of his need to stand alone and possess his own soul. And this, it appears to me, is the significance of the episode in the novel.[2]

---

[2] It is interesting to note to what lengths critics sometimes go in their efforts to invent plausible explanations for an incident or episode in a Lawrence novel whose inclusion they cannot justify on artistic grounds but which is, nevertheless, too

The theme of aloneness also serves to link Aaron with Rawdon Lilly. The close connection between the conceptions of the characters of Aaron and Lilly has often been commented on. J. M. Murry, reviewing *Aaron's Rod,* remarked that "Aaron is the instinct to which Lilly supplies the consciousness." Horace Gregory refers to Aaron and Lilly as two contradicting elements within Lawrence himself. F. R. Leavis sees Aaron as "an *alter-ego*" and his questioning of Lilly as "something very like a *dialogue intérieur.*" There is no doubt a great deal of truth in these remarks, though one must beware of taking them too literally. All that Lilly says in the novel about love, marriage, power, and possession of one's soul is, we might say, a total proposition which is put to the test in the novel. Parts of it find ready approval from other characters, and one gets the impression that the reader is also expected to concur; but certain other parts are looked at with suspicion by Aaron, and these he is unwilling to accept. The reader, I take it, is also meant to take them in this light and see these views of Lilly's for what they are. The novel, in any case, presents both a case and its criticism—though as I shall have occasion to say, the criticism is not strong enough for the book to be an artistically satisfying whole.

We find Lilly first of all enlarging on the theme of love in an argument with Jim Bricknell which, for the former, ends with "a punch in the wind." Jim complains that he is going to pieces, that life is leaving him because he has no one to love him. He believes that "Love is life," and that the highest a man is capable of is to sacrifice himself to love. To this Lilly replies by saying that what Jim calls love is actually a vice, "a sheer ignominy;" and that it is not the lack of love but the craving for love and self-sacrifice on Jim's part which makes him feel he is losing life. "You should stand by yourself and learn to be yourself," he tells him. These remarks by Lilly—which are elaborated in great detail in the course of the novel, especially in Lilly's conversations with Aaron—bear a direct relevance to Aaron's case. Aaron, too, like Jim, had at one time believed that the final consummation for him

---

prominent and challenging to be simply ignored. F. R. Leavis, for instance, finds the Aaron-Marchesa episode "irritatingly unsatisfying" because it seems to him not completely significant. There is no inevitability, he says, about the episode as a part of Aaron's history. He, therefore, confidently concludes that it appears in the novel because "Lawrence himself had encountered the original of the Marchesa and been struck by her—been intrigued by her interest as a case." J. I. M. Stewart, who also fails to see the significance of the episode for Aaron's story, dismisses it as "no more than one of those routine conquests of high-born ladies by proletarian lovers which it gave [Lawrence] pleasure to invent."

lay in sacrificing himself to love, forgetting that the self is greater than love. He, too, had mistaken the process of love for a goal.

> The aim of any process is not the perpetuation of that process, but the completion thereof. Love is a process of the incomprehensible human soul: love also incomprehensible, but still only a process. The process should work to a completion, not to some horror of intensification and extremity wherein the soul and body ultimately perish. The completion of the process of love is the arrival at a state of simple, pure self-possession, for man and woman. Only that. Which isn't exciting enough for us sensationalists. We prefer abysses and maudlin self-abandon and self-sacrifice, the degeneration into a sort of slime and merge.
>
> Perhaps, truly, the process of love is never accomplished. But it moves in great stages, and at the end of each stage a true goal, where the soul possesses itself in simple and generous singleness.

Lilly firmly believes that before men and women can come together they must, in the first place, learn to stand by themselves, for "nothing is any good unless each stands alone, intrinsically." He also holds that the relationship of marriage—which he calls *egoisme à deux*—should be extended, or re-adjusted, so that man can stand on his own legs and, uniting with other men, can bring back the spirit of adventure in life. Graham Hough has expressed his doubts on the point, and his reading of what he calls "the queer semi-amorous wranglings between Aaron and Lilly" in Chapter X leads him to the conclusion that "they are looking for a substitute for marriage rather than a solution of its problems." A similar point has also been made by H. M. Daleski in his recent book on Lawrence. Such a view might be mistakenly seen to be substantiated by the scene where Lilly brings the flu-sticken Aaron to his room and, finding that he is sulking himself out of life, massages his lower body with oil "as mothers do their babies whose bowels don't work:"

> For a long time he rubbed finely and steadily, then went over the whole of the lower body, mindless, as if in a sort of incantation. He rubbed every speck of the man's lower body—the abdomen, the buttocks, the thighs and knees, down to his feet, rubbed it all warm and glowing with camphorated oil, every bit of it, chafing the toes swiftly, till he was almost exhausted. Then Aaron was covered up again, and Lilly sat down in fatigue to look at his patient.

An attentive reading of the whole scene would, however, make it obvious that it is these personal contacts with other men based on love, sympathy, or sacrifice, that Lilly is moving away from. As he nurses Aaron, he is reminded of his wife Tanny's final remark after he had received a punch in the wind from Jim Bricknell: "You shouldn't try to make a little Jesus of yourself, coming so near to people, wanting to help them." Now he reflects that as soon as Aaron is better he, too, would probably give him a punch in the wind, metaphorically if not literally, for having interfered with him. A Jesus, he concludes, makes a Judas inevitable. Hence his decision: "All right, Aaron. Last time I break my bread for anybody, this is. So get better, my flautist, so that I can go away." The conclusion that the impersonal, purposive relationship with other men that Lilly is seeking is presented "suspiciously like an alternative to marriage" is belied by the entire argument of the novel. Lilly makes it quite clear in the very first extended conversation he has with Aaron that when he speaks of man's learning to possess his own soul in patience and in peace, he does not have anything like a negative Nirvana in mind. It is a state in which one does not cease to love, or even to hate: in fact one can come to attain this state only "after a lot of fighting and a lot of sensual fulfilment. And it never does away with the fighting and with the sensual passion. It flowers on top of them, and it would never flower save on top of them." It is thus obvious that the very basis of man's possessing his own soul in fullness is assumed to be a satisfactory sensual fulfilment in marriage. Moreover, a man can be best alone and at peace only when his woman has also accomplished for herself the possession of her own soul. This is, Lilly tells Aaron, what he is hoping for in his own relationship with his wife:

> ". . . And if Tanny possesses her own soul in patience and peace as well—and if in this we understand each other at last—then there we are, together and apart at the same time, and free of each other, and eternally inseparable." . . . "You learn to be quite alone and possess your own soul in isolation—and at the same time to be perfectly *with* someone else—That's all I ask."

As Lilly explains in a subsequent conversation, in being "quite alone" a man does not choose to be sentimental or lonely; he merely learns, by choice, to be what by his own nature he essentially is. In as much as he is a single individual soul he *is, ipso facto,* alone. "In so far as I am I, and only I am I, and I am only I, in so far, I am inevitably and eternally alone, and it is my last blessedness to know it, and to accept it, and to live with this as the core of my self-knowledge."

Aaron can see that Lilly has, largely, learned to be alone with his own soul, and is even envious of him. He himself, he feels, cannot yet stand by himself in the middle of the world with nothing to hold on to. In one way the whole of Aaron's story develops round his efforts to acquire the ability to stand alone and be in possession of his own soul.[3] When he first hears Lilly talk glibly—as it seems to him—of possessing one's soul in patience and in peace, he is provoked to retort back—and the retort is a comment on his condition at the time—that in actual life one possesses one's soul neither in patience nor in peace, "but any devil that likes possesses you and does what it likes with you, while you fridge yourself and fray yourself out like a worn rag." Lilly's words, however, remain with him and he is reminded of them a long time afterward following the disillusion of his experience with the Marchesa. His instinctive reaction is one of deep hatred toward her, but he says to himself: "No, I won't hate her. I won't hate her." Realizing that he must learn to be in possession of himself, he refuses to follow the "reflex of his own passion" and decides that he is not going to feel bitter toward the Marchesa—seeing also that "she too was struggling with her fate" and had been nothing but generous toward him. This he does, we are told, "under the influence of Lilly." With Lilly's help he also comes to understand, in part, his own position. Lilly explains to him in the last chapter of the book—entitled appropriately, and perhaps not without a touch of irony as well, "Words"—that his first and last responsibility is to his own self:

> ". . . You *are* yourself and so *be* yourself. Stick to it and abide by it. Passion or no passion, ecstasy or no ecstasy, urge or no urge, there's no goal outside you, where you can consum[m]ate like an eagle flying into the sun, or a moth into a candle. . . .

[3] Julian Moynahan, who thinks differently, takes the following entertainingly "competent" view of Aaron's quest, adding some speculations on his future, to boot: "On a hard view, and in the end the novel forces this view on all except the most incompetent of Lawrence's readers, Aaron, like the majority of the twenty thousand American men who take the option of a poor man's divorce each year, deserts his family simply out of boredom. He becomes a plaything of the idle rich, peddling his musical talent and sexual magnetism to neurotic upper-class wives and mistresses in exchange for more or less luxurious lodgings, fees, and sensations. He exploits the appetite of a jaded social set for queer birds and can be expected to go on drifting until his luck runs out with the onset of age and the decline of his novelty value. It is hard to imagine what he might be doing in twenty-five years' time. Perhaps if Italy continued to suit his indolent disposition he might be found improvising a musical background to speeches delivered over the Italian radio by Ezra Pound." . . .

"There is only one thing, your own very self. So you'd better
stick to it. . . . You've got one job, and no more. There inside you
lies your own very self, like a germinating egg, . . . and since it is the
only thing you have got or ever will have, don't go trying to lose it.
You've got to develop it, from the egg into the chicken, and from the
chicken into the one-and-only phoenix, of which there can only be
one at a time in the universe. . . . Your own single oneness is your
destiny. Your destiny comes from within, from your own self-form.
And you can't know it beforehand, neither your destiny nor your
self-form. You can only develop it. You can only stick to your own
very self, and *never* betray it. . . ."

Since the destiny one has to unfold comes from within, one must—
Lilly's "flood of words" goes on—fulfill one's soul's impulse, whatever the impulse be. If the soul urges one to love, one must love.
"If you've got to go in for love and passion, go in for them," he
tells Aaron. But he also exhorts him to remember that love and
passion are not the goal but only a means—the only goal being the
fulfillment of one's own soul's active desire and suggestion. To
all this Aaron does not object. He also agrees that to make love
the supreme urge, or to assert that "love and love alone must rule"
is "all a lie." But when Lilly goes on to expound his views on power,
and to contend that in the mode of power woman must submit
in a "deep, unfathomable free submission" to man, Aaron cannot
acquiesce. He, to begin with, does not attach to power-urge the
kind of significance given to it by Lilly. "I don't see power as so
very important," he tells him. Moreover, despite Lilly's insistence,
he cannot believe that woman will ever yield to what Lilly calls
"the positive power-soul in man." Lilly goes on to suggest that
Aaron himself has the need to yield submission "to the heroic soul
in a greater man." The novel ends rather inconclusively with Lilly's
words to Aaron that his own soul will tell him to whom he should
submit. The ending—which leaves the theme of power to be
treated more adequately and comprehensively in the next two
novels, *Kangaroo* and *The Plumed Serpent*—seems to me quite
appropriate: but in handing over nearly all of the last "Words"
chapter to Lilly, Lawrence, I think, failed to include in the book
adequate criticism of Lilly's point of view. This is a serious flaw
in *Aaron's Rod,* and in this respect it is probably the weakest of
Lawrence's mature novels.

Anthony Beal
On Kangaroo

In . . . *Kangaroo,* the setting is Australia. Frieda is with Lawrence again and the two appear practically undisguised as the Somers and Harriet of the novel. There is an autumnal aura about their marriage: sex is quiescent and we are even informed that they occupy separate bedrooms. Tribute is paid to Harriet's "gay, undying courage, her wonderful fresh zest in front of life"; but there is some bitter argument between the two, centring on the man's need for some relation with other people, beyond marriage.

One is made to realize how desperately isolated Somers-Lawrence is in the world: he is set apart from his fellow men, a wanderer on the face of the earth with no job, no children, and no place in society. All he has is his wife, and he "knew that her greatest grief was when he turned away from their personal human life intimacy to this impersonal business of male activity for which he was always craving." He has a terrible dream in which the two people he had loved—his wife and mother—combine into one woman who accuses him of betraying her love for him. They had both believed in him terribly, in personal being. "But in the impersonal man, a man that would go beyond them, with his back to them, away from them into an activity that excluded them, in this man they did not find it so easy to believe."

But Somers-Lawrence desperately needs this further life:

> "I want to do something with living people, somewhere, somehow, while I live on the earth. I write, but I write alone. And I live alone. Without any connection whatever with the rest of men."

Harriet retorts that his writing is enough "doing." She is scornful of his other aspirations. She knows that he will only be disappointed in his efforts for mankind, and then turn back again to her. In his heart of hearts Somers knows she is right, but he still feels the desire to be a leader, to make one final attempt to influence men by action.

From D. H. Lawrence *by Anthony Beal. Oliver & Boyd Ltd., 1961. Reprinted by permission.*

Somers is a much more attractive person than Lilly. The strident and rather ridiculous figure in *Aaron's Rod* is here replaced by an odd and appealing, sometimes almost pathetic, little man (his littleness is emphasized) who possesses some of "the magic of the old world, . . . the old culture, the old glamour."

"A comical-looking bloke! Perhaps a Bolshie." So a Sydney workman describes him on the first page of the novel, and the remark sheds light both on Somers and on Australians. To Lawrence a new country is always far more than just the scenery, wonderfully though he will render that: it is the feel of the place, above all the way the people live, that interests him. The Australian ambience is powerfully invoked and dramatically presented from the very first paragraph of the book: the lack of subtlety, the free and easy casualness which ends either in profound indifference or in sheer take-it-or-leave-it "bloody-mindedness." In this relaxed atmosphere the Somerses settle in at their suburban bungalow and gradually become friendly with the couple next door, Jack and Victoria Calcott. There is some lively description of middle-class suburban life. Jack tells Somers of the movement in which he is involved—an organization of ex-servicemen's clubs, the "Diggers," ostensibly social and athletic, but secretly organized on semi-military lines, aiming at revolution and the seizure of power. The head of the movement is a Jewish lawyer in Sydney, known as Kangaroo.

Kangaroo is one of Lawrence's most ambitious attempts at creating a male character who is not at all like Lawrence himself. We know that no such man and no such political movement existed in Australia at the time. Both were invented by Lawrence as dramatizations of the sort of political leader and movement with which he might usefully work. One cannot imagine him participating in the traditional English political system, nor indeed can one see him giving his whole-hearted allegience to any conventional established party. The Diggers' movement is rather contrived; as far as one can see, their only reason for wanting a revolution is that they crave excitement and "are dying for another scrap." Kangaroo himself is unlike any obvious dictator, and his idea of the new society that the revolution will bring about is extremely sketchy—a sort of wise and benevolent despotism. But the man is powerfully presented, alternatively grotesque and beautiful, loving and ferocious: in him Lawrence creates the strong opponent-friend for his hero that was so lacking in *Aaron's Rod*.

The personal love-hate relationship between Somers and Kangaroo is dramatically worked out. But Somers-Lawrence is not really concerned any more with the idea of conjunction between two men; and while he is interested in the possibility of political action changing the present, he is sceptical about its effect on the future:

> "Sometimes I feel I'd give anything, soul and body, for a smash-up in this social-industrial world we're in. And I would. And then when I realise people—just people—the same people after it as before—why then I don't care any more, and feel it's time to turn to the gods."

The last phrase reveals the new interest that is now growing in Lawrence—no longer women, no longer men, no longer political power—but "the gods." For the time being, however, he is still sufficiently fascinated by politics to extend Somers' experiences to include the socialist rivals of Kangaroo's faction. He meets Willie Struthers, a labor leader, who wants to enlist his services and offers him the editorship of a socialist paper. Somers is "touched on one of his quivering strings" by Struthers' appeal to his working-class feelings, the appeal to the "love of a man for his mate." But he rejects it: absolute love for "a mate" would be as fatal as absolute love for a woman. "When human love starts out to lock individuals together, it is just courting disaster."

He leaves Struthers to go straight to Kangaroo and tell him much the same thing: "Don't love me. Don't want me to love you. Let's be hard separate men." At this, Kangaroo becomes hideous and malignant, threatens Somers and orders him to leave the country. Somers, absolutely terrified, with Kangaroo following "slowly, awfully, behind, like a mad man," manages to escape from the house, and walks out into the Sydney streets in fear.

The story has moved forward with reasonable momentum through two hundred pages to this climax of terror. The atmosphere of conspiracy and fear and malignity around the rival leaders is conveyed with some of the force found in Conrad's political novels. Lawrence has built up a situation of physical excitement, rare in his novels. What will happen to Somers? Will he be killed? or driven out of the country? We turn expectantly to the next chapter, "The Nightmare," and find—total collapse.

For the next fifty pages the story is forgotten, and Australia is not even mentioned. Instead, we are given pure Lawrencian autobiography—more direct and circumstantial than in *Sons and Lovers*—with nothing changed but the people's names. It is an account of Frieda's and Lawrence's life during the 1914–18 War. Lawrence did not mention the War in the novels which he wrote

when it was actually in progress, but now, three or four years after
it had ended, he feels an overwhelming need to let out the pent-
up feelings that it aroused in him. So ironically, in this Australian
fiction, the most violent emotions presented are those actually
experienced in wartime England by Lawrence himself, "one of
the most intensely English little men England ever produced."

As we have seen, what really shocked Lawrence about the
War was not the tragic waste, the horror and futility of the carn-
age; it was what he regarded as the invasion of his privacy, the
desire of the authorities to "humiliate him as a separate, single
man. . . ." The following passage is symptomatic:

> Oh, foul dogs. But they were very close on him now, very close. They
> were grinning very close behind him, like hyenas just going to bite.
> Yes, they were running him to earth. They had exposed all his naked-
> ness to gibes. And they were pining, almost whimpering to give the
> last grab at him, and haul him to earth, a victim. Finished! But not yet!
> Oh, no, not yet. Not yet, not now, nor ever. Not while life was life,
> should they lay hold of him. Never again. Never would he be touched
> again. And because they had handled his private parts, and looked
> into them, their eyes should burst and their hands should wither and
> their hearts should rot. So he cursed them in his blood, with an un-
> remitting curse, as he waited.

This outburst was occasioned by a perfectly routine medical examination which Lawrence had (in common with every other man
of military age in the country) to see if he were fit for service.
This hysterical fury illustrates in an extreme form the central
passion in Lawrence's life, *the desire to be left alone.*

He had, in fact, a great deal to be bitter about during the
War—ill-health, dire poverty, the banning of *The Rainbow,* and
subsequent difficulty in getting his other work published. All this
he bore with stoicism and courage. Yet he went half-crazy about a
medical examination and about an imagined persecution campaign
on a vast scale to bring him to "the heel of a Jewish financier."
One may feel that this does no credit to his intelligence. He himself
admits that it was "irrational," but "there is no arguing with the
instinctive passional self."

It has been claimed that this long autobiographical diversion
is an integral part of the structure of the novel, because it sheds
light on Somers-Lawrence's thoughts and feelings about society
and politics. Obviously there is a continuum between Lawrence in
wartime England and Lawrence in Australia a few years later;
but if all that was required was to give some background depth to

the present Somers, Lawrence could have done this in a few pages
(as he gave the background of Gerald Crich in *Women in Love*)
without disrupting the story at its most critical part. But quite obviously Lawrence is here in the grip of a compulsive need to retell
this nightmare experience in his past—and the strength of the need
may be judged from the difficulty he finds in getting back to his
story.

Even when he was worked finally through the war experiences
and their effect on him, there is a chapter called "Bits" which
consists literally of bits from the Sydney *Bulletin,* interspersed with
bits of scenery and bits of preaching. "This gramophone of a
novel," he calls it; and a page or two later we are back to "dear
reader" stuff (in the worst style of *Aaron's Rod*), while the next
chapter begins: "Chapter follows chapter and nothing doing."
By this time seventy pages have passed since we left Somers walking the Sydney streets in fear after the escape from Kangaroo.
The impetus of the story has been completely lost; but it comes to
life again for one dramatic episode. There is a great Labour rally
in Sydney that Somers attends; as Willie Struthers addresses it,
a riot organized by Kangaroo's Diggers breaks out. Shots are fired,
a bomb is thrown—and Kangaroo is mortally wounded. On his
deathbed he pleads with Somers to tell him that he loves him, but
Somers cannot bring himself to tell this lie. So Kangaroo dies in
the prime of life, fulfilled neither through his political aims nor
through his love for Somers.

It is also the end of Somers-Lawrence's dream of action and
leadership in the world of men. However important the world of
men and the great human loves for wife, child or comrade, "something else was true at the same time. Man's isolation was always a
supreme truth and fact, not to be forsworn. And the mystery of
apartness. And the greater mystery of the dark God beyond a
man. . . ."

Despite the disruption of the story, there is a coherent progression of thought and belief throughout the book. Lawrence
begins with the need for some connexion with the world of men—
the old dream of the artist to be a man of action—and finds this
ambition running counter to the wife's demand for a purely personal life. Then comes the realization that political action is use-
less because, although it may change events, it does not change
men; then re-affirmation of the supreme importance of the individual; and, lastly, the newly-expressed belief in the "dark gods."
Lawrence does little to define the dark gods. They are "forever
unrealisable," their medium is the profound unconscious, and they

are the complete antithesis of the spiritual-ideal, possessively loving God of Christianity, who is a "proposition of the mental consciousness."

Australia acts as a counterpoint to these main themes. As ever, Lawrence's feelings for a new place have all the fluctuations and contradictions of his feelings for another person. So, when he first arrives in Sydney, we find him, rather incredibly, pining for London Bridge, St. Martin's Lane and Westminster. But by the end of the book he is rejecting Europe and its "huge ponderous cathedrals and factories and cities," and loving the "uncreatedness" of the Australian landscape, both man-made and natural:

> Since that day he had been thankful for the amorphous scrappy scattering of foundationless shacks and bungalows. Since then he had loved the Australian landscape, with the remote gum trees running their white nerves into the air, the random streets of flimsy bungalows, all loose from one another, and temporary seeming, the bungalows perched precariously on the knolls, like Japanese paper-houses, below the ridge of wire-and-tuft trees . . . the flimsy hills of Australia were like a new world, and the frail *inconspicuousness* of the landscape, that was still so clear and clean, clean of all fogginess or confusion: but the frail, aloof, inconspicuous clarity of the landscape was like a sort of heaven—bungalows, shacks, corrugated iron and all.

Kangaroo contains some of Lawrence's most brilliant natural description—pictures of small towns, of Sydney Harbor, of the Pacific coast, of the bush, and of the onset of an Australian spring. These have a freshness and lyricism reminiscent of *The White Peacock,* but at the same time all the power of Lawrence's mature art. Yet, despite his delight in the beauty of Australia, the "absolute necessity to move" is on Somers-Lawrence again; and the book ends with him (and Harriet-Frieda) sailing for America, "which seemed to lie next in his line of destiny."

Keith Sagar
The Lost Train: The Plumed Serpent

The Plumed Serpent has been mauled by the critics from Frieda, who called it "desiccated swelled head," onward. Any critic might be expected to have reservations about this novel, but the wholesale condemnation it has received is indicative, it seems to me, of far deeper failings in the critics than in the book; a failure in imaginative range and flexibility; a failure to meet the basic critical challenge, the challenge to enter wholly, if only temporarily, into the fictional world. Critics have kept the book at arms' length, with an almost hysterical defensiveness, as if it were not art but propaganda. Indeed, this very charge has been often made. I do not wish for a moment to argue that Lawrence does not expect his readers to take Don Ramon's programme perfectly seriously: "I do mean what Ramon means—for all of us," only that this programme has been grossly misrepresented and is, in any case, fully embodied as art within a larger complex structure, a structure controlled not by Ramon but by Kate.

The novel has been fortunate in its more recent critics. Jascha Kessler, John B. Vickery and, particularly, L. D. Clark, have testified most persuasively to its coherence as art, stressing Kate's mythic quest for a source of renewal. She undergoes a spiritual death, receives and responds to a call, finds herself in strange territory with horrors, but also glimpses of a deeper reality (in visions and visitations), struggles in the death-throes of the old way, the old consciousness, the strings which bind to the old life, does not, like the great mythic heroes, then return to the world renewed and bringing renewal (as the man who died is to do), but is left at the end still standing outside her own mythic role, testing and testing it against her conscience and the realities of her experience, testing these in turn against the new life. For Lawrence is not preaching, he is using the novel to explore the possibilities of experience. Is Don Ramon's trail the right one: for him? for Mexico? for Kate?

This structure differs from that of *The Woman Who Rode*

From The Art of D. H. Lawrence *by K. M. Sagar. Cambridge University Press, 1966. Reprinted by permission.*

Away in that Ramon and Cipriano are by no means primitive Indians (and it is to them rather than to their cult that she gives her allegiance, though she respects and is sympathetic toward what they are trying to do), and in that Kate does not passively submit, but fights her own transformation every step of the way.

Kate does not really know why she has come to Mexico, except that

> over in England, in Ireland, in Europe, she had heard the *consummatum est* of her own spirit. It was finished, in a kind of death agony.

She had lived, until recently, through her love for her husband, Joachim, who had died, broken in his efforts to do something for Ireland. Joachim is clearly Lawrence* who had almost broken himself trying to do something for England, but had now decided to turn away from Europe altogether to seek the old gods. When she quotes Joachim she is quoting Lawrence himself:

> Joachim said that evil was the lapsing back to old life-modes that have been surpassed in us.

But her instinct to believe drives her to defend Don Ramon against Joachim:

> No! It's not a helpless, panic reversal. It is conscious, carefully chosen. We must go back to pick up old threads. We must take up the old, broken impulse that will connect us with the mystery of the cosmos again, now we are at the end of our own tether.

Mexico itself certainly offers no hope to Kate or anyone else. The shedding of blood, however inhuman, had been a meaningful act for the Aztecs; but the spilling of blood and bowels in the Mexico bull-ring is obscenely gratuitous, an expression of the corruption and cowardice of those who performed and those who applauded. The first chapter closes with one of the book's central images:

> She felt again, as she felt before, that Mexico lay in her destiny almost as a doom. Something so heavy, so oppressive, like the folds of some huge serpent that seemed as if it could hardly raise itself.

* Joachim if he is anyone is probably John Middleton Murry. (Joachim = John; Katherine = Kate). [*ed. note*]

People and place alike seem characterized by ugliness, squalid evil, brutality, jeering malevolence:

> There was a ponderous, down-pressing weight upon the spirit: the great folds of the dragon of the Aztecs, the dragon of the Toltecs winding around one and weighing down the soul.

> Perhaps something came out of the earth, the dragon of the earth, some effluence, some vibration which militated against the very composition of the blood and nerves in human beings.

How can this serpent, this "dragon of degenerate or of incomplete existence" be transformed into the living Quetzalcoatl of Don Ramon's pantheon? Apparently the Aztecs themselves began the degeneration when they "raised their deity to heights of horror and vindictiveness." And underneath the Catholicism of modern Mexico is a "profound unbelief" which has made the dragon still more malevolent, still more of a burden, a constricting inertia, strangling life. If Don Ramon can restore belief by resurrecting Quetzalcoatl as a young and shining god, the dragon will raise himself and resume his good aspect.

Ruskin described the snake as "a divine hieroglyph of the demoniac power of the earth—of the entire earthly Nature." It is exactly in this sense that Lawrence's snake functions in its mythic status, a status which he later enlarged upon in *Etruscan Places:*

> In the old world the centre of all power was at the depths of the earth, and at the depths of the sea, while the sun was only a moving subsidiary body: and . . . the serpent represented the vivid powers of the inner earth, not only such powers as volcanic and earthquake, but the quick powers that run up the roots of plants and establish the great body of the tree, the tree of life, and run up the feet and legs of man, to establish the heart.

In *Apocalypse* Lawrence goes on to discuss the "half-divine half-demonish nature" of the potency for which the snake stands:

> It is this which surges in us to make us move, to make us act, to make us bring forth something: to make us spring up and live. Modern philosophers may call it Libido or *Elan Vital,* but the words are thin, they carry none of the wild suggestion of the dragon.

His coils within the sun make the sun glad, till the sun dances in radiance. For in his good aspect, the dragon is the great vivifier, the great enhancer of the whole universe.

The plumed serpent is compounded of snake and eagle. It is the eagle who is held to demand blood-sacrifice to the sun whence he comes:

> The eagle flies nearest to the sun, no other bird flies so near. So he brings down the life of the sun, and the power of the sun, in his wings, and men who see him wheeling are filled with the elation of the sun. But all creatures of the sun must dip their mouths in blood, the sun is for ever thirsty, thirsting for the brightest exhalation of blood.

Quetzalcoatl is a phoenix, for he threw himself into a volcano when Christ came to Mexico, and so ascended as smoke to the place behind the sun where the gods live, there to sleep the great sleep of regeneration until his cycle should come round.

It is not, however, as a plumed serpent that Quetzalcoatl manifests himself, but as a man of great stature, dark and bearded, his body shining like gold, who rises naked from the Lake of Sayula. It is the newspaper article reporting this supposed event which acts as Kate's call:

> Strangely, a different light than the common light seemed to gleam out of the words of even this newspaper paragraph. . . . Quetzalcoatl was, she vaguely remembered, a sort of fair-faced bearded god; the wind, the breath of life, the eyes that see and are unseen, like the stars by day.

The experience of reading this paragraph affects Kate much as the cell under the microscope or the final rainbow had affected Ursula:

> Amid all the bitterness that Mexico produced in her spirit, there was still a strange beam of wonder and mystery, almost like hope. A strange darkly-iridescent beam of wonder, of magic. . . .
> Gods should be iridescent, like the rainbow in the storm. . . . Gods die with men who have conceived them. But the god-stuff roars eternally, like the sea, with too vast a sound to be heard.

The rainbow signified the arc of the covenant between man and God, the guarantee of continuing creative intercourse, primarily between heaven and earth, by rain and sunshine. The Quetzal-coatl symbol, a snake with his tail in his mouth, the markings on his back forming the rays of a sun within which an eagle spreads his wings, signifies also this covenant and this intercourse, so that the rituals center on the coming of the rains, and the men of Quetzalcoatl call themselves Lords of the Two Ways, of heaven and earth, fire and water, day and night. Quetzalcoatl is also Lord of the Morning Star, because he stands between the day and the night, in the creative twilight, time of rebirth. His return is the return of Pan, or Lucifer in all his pristine brightness:

> Lucifer is brighter now than tarnished Michael or shabby Gabriel. All things fall in their turn, now Michael goes down, and whispering Gabriel, and the Son of the Morning will laugh at them all. Yes, I am all for Lucifer, who is really the Morning Star. (Frieda, *Not I But the Wind*)

The Morning Star is also the Soul-star, the spark, "the Quick of all beings and existence, which he called the Morning Star, since men must give all things names." And it is the meeting-ground, the sacrament, in all creative human relationships. It is Don Ramon's self-appointed task to transform the fanged serpent of the horror of Mexico into this new and ancient god, who is but a manifestation of the godhead within all living things:

> Quetzalcoatl is to me only the symbol of the best a man may be, in the next days. The universe is a nest of dragons, with a perfectly unfathomable life-mystery at the centre of it. If I call the mystery the Morning Star, surely it doesn't matter! A man's blood can't beat in the abstract.

Don Ramon comes very close to those modern Christians who call their God not the Morning Star, but "the infinite and inex-haustible depth and ground of all being" (Tillich). John Robinson, in *Honest to God,* quotes Bonhoeffer's definition of God as "the 'beyond' in the midst of our life, . . . not on the borders of life, but at its center." He also quotes Don Ramon:

> And then—when you find your own manhood—your womanhood, . . . then you know it is not your own, to do as you like with. You don't have it of your own will. It comes from—from the middle—from the God. Beyond me, at the middle, is the God.

Don Ramon later tells his son:

I believe that the hearts of living men are the very middle of the sky.
And there God is; and Paradise; inside the hearts of living men and
women.

When Kate, through the words of the newspaper, hears "the
soundless call, across all the hideous choking" she knows why she
has come to Mexico:

> To be alone with the unfolding flower of her own soul, in the delicate,
> chiming silence that is at the midst of things.

She recognizes in Don Ramon and Cipriano "men face to face
not with death and self-sacrifice, but with the life-issue." She is
drawn to the magic Lake of Sayula, and finds there that the horror
and heaviness of the atmosphere of Mexico for the first time re-
laxes. Another spirit emanates from the "sperm-like" waters of the
lake. The lake is sacred to the oldest gods and offerings were
thrown into it by the ancients. The lake is the center of the new
world, the bath of life, the mixing-bowl. A man emerges from the
water to demand tribute to Quetzalcoatl. In his face, and that of
the crippled boatman, her Charon, she sees

> a look of extraordinary, arresting beauty, the silent, vulnerable centre
> of all life's quivering, like the nucleus gleaming in tranquil suspense,
> within a cell.

As they part, the boatman gives her a token, an ollita, a little
earthenware pot from the time of the old gods, which he fishes
from the bed of the lake. This is the beginning of Kate's initiation.
    Only a miracle could save Mexico, Don Ramon had told Kate,
but "the miracle is always there . . . for the man who can pass his
hand through to it, to take it." Kate touches it when she says
"Come then!" to "the silent life-breath which hung unrevealed in
the atmosphere, waiting." What she submits to here is not the
horror, but what she takes to be its opposite, the promise of fulfilment, a power which will help her to build herself, to win her
soul out of the chaos:

> In her soul she was thinking of the communion of grace. With the
> black-eyed man it was the same. He was humbler. But as he peeled
> his orange and dropped the yellow peel on the water, she could see
> the stillness, the humility, and the pathos of grace in him; something
> very beautiful and truly male, and very hard to find in a civilised white
> man. It was not of the spirit. It was of the dark, strong, unbroken
> blood, the flowering of the soul.

The Morning Star is "the gleaming clue to the two opposites," but not the opposites of blood-knowledge and mental consciousness, soul and spirit:

> But down on it all, like a weight of obsidian, comes the passive negation of the Indian. He understands soul, which is of the blood. But spirit, which is superior, and is the quality of our civilisation, this, in the mass, he darkly and barbarically repudiates.

> Kate was attracted and repelled. She was attracted, almost fascinated by the strange nuclear power of the men in the circle. It was like a darkly glowing, vivid nucleus of new life. Repellant the strange heaviness, the sinking of the spirit into the earth, like dark water. Repellant the silent, dense opposition to the pale-faced spiritual direction. Yet here and here alone, it seemed to her, life burned with a deep new fire. . . . Surely this was a new kindling of mankind!

Or is it merely a new kindling of old lusts?

> It was not that their eyes were exactly fierce. But their blackness was inchoate, with a dagger of white light in it. And in the inchoate blackness the blood-lust might arise, out of the sediment of the uncreated past. . . . They are caught in the toils of old lusts and old activities as in the folds of a black serpent that strangles the heart. . . . So, these men, unable to overcome the elements, men held down by the serpent tangle of sun and electricity and volcanic emission, they are subject to an ever-recurring, fathomless lust of resentment, a demonish hatred of life itself. Then, the instriking thud of a heavy knife, stabbing into a living body, this is the best. No lust of woman can equal that lust. The clutching throb of gratification as the knife strikes in and the blood spurts out!

In his efforts to transform this "black serpent that strangles the heart" into a fine new god who can redeem a murderous people, Don Ramon can hardly change the elements of Mexico. He cannot push Mexico toward Europe. He must come to terms with the old lusts and old activities, with a race which will never come forth from its own darkness into "the upper world of daylight and fresh air," never be "frank" and "open," never see that other creatures have lives of their own, to be respected, as one's own life is to be respected. He knows that blood-lust itself must be satisfied by offering up the blood of defeated enemies to the sun. In fact the men Don Ramon executes would have been executed by normal processes of law in most countries today (as L. D. Clark has pointed out). It is rather in the power and licence he gives to Cipriano that Don Ramon compromises with the horror:

If it seemed to him a knave, a treacherous cur, he stabbed him to the heart, saying: "I am the red Huitzilopochtli, of the knife."

Cipriano openly embraces the horror:

Why not? Horror is real. . . . The bit of horror is like the sesame seed in the nougat, it gives the sharp wild flavour. It is good to have it there.

What Don Ramon offers Kate is a dream of innocence regained:

When great plains stretched away to the oceans, like Atlantis and the lost continents of Polynesia, so that seas were only great lakes, and the soft, dark-eyed people of that world could walk around the globe. Then there was a mysterious, hot-blooded, soft-footed humanity with a strange civilisation of its own.

The "mental-spiritual life of white people" is quickly withering and will soon die. But Kate, drawing on the mysticism and potency of the aboriginal Celtic people at the bottom of her soul, can then help to bring about

a new germ, a new conception of human life, that will arise from the fusion of the old blood-and-vertebrate consciousness with the white man's present mental-spiritual consciousness. The sinking of both beings into a new being.

She sees her marriage in these terms: "the marriage which is the only step to the new world of man." But she is here affirming a position very different from Don Ramon's. He will have no truck with the mental-spiritual consciousness. His rituals are entirely devoted to the blood-and-vertebrate consciousness to the exclusion of mind. He marries a woman who, unlike Kate, will totally submit to him; and he calls Kate renegade when she proposes to return to Europe.

Kate's own standards of balance, "fusion," demand that she should retain some independence, not submit wholly. Yet Cipriano, in his role as Pan, as demon lover, enforces such a submission to his "great pliant column," his "huge erection":

Submission absolute, like the earth under the sky. Beneath an overarching absolute.

This terrible, complete marriage offers her passivity and abandon, the abandoning of everything, including her own selfhood:

> Her world could end in many ways, and this was one of them. Back to the twilight of the ancient Pan world, where the soul of the woman was dumb, to be forever unspoken.

Is this not, by her own standards and Lawrence's, truly renegade? Is it not a reversal of Ursula's painful struggle toward selfhood and articulation, back to the uncreated surcharged consciousness of the early Brangwens? Is not the denial that one alone can have a soul—"It takes a man and a woman together to make a soul"— a denial of the star-polarity Birkin and Ursula found in marriage? This is the terrible price Kate has to pay for her abandon:

> What do I care if he kills people? His flame is young and clean. He is Huitzilopochtli, and I am Malintzi. What do I care, what Cipriano Viedma does or doesn't do? Or even what Kate Leslie does or doesn't do!

Her marriage to Cipriano is clearly seen by the novel as equivalent to the death of the woman who rode away: "Was this the knife to which she must be sheath?"

What holds Kate in Mexico at the end is not her belief in Don Ramon's "high-flown bunk," not her own belief in the fusion of the two types of consciousness, not even her own submergence in the older consciousness she occasionally experiences, but the man, Cipriano, who must take her to give her life, at forty, some meaning, and prevent her deterioration into another Mrs. Witt.

> Ramon and Cipriano no doubt were right for themselves, for their people and country. But for herself, ultimately, ultimately she belonged elsewhere.

In the last chapter Mexico softens for her. The peons loading a spangled bull into a ship's hold are the opposite of the obscene bullfighters of the opening chapter. The peon with the baby donkey is the opposite of the urchin who tortured the water-fowl:

> Glancing up, Kate met again the peon's eyes, with their black, full flame of life heavy with knowledge and with a curious reassurance. The black foal, the mother, the drinking, the new life, the mystery of the shadowy battlefield of creation; and the adoration of

the full-breasted, glorious woman beyond him: all this seemed in the
primitive black eyes of the man.

"Adios!" said Kate to him, lingeringly.

"Adios, Patrona!" he replied, suddenly lifting his hand high, in
the Quetzalcoatl salute.

But the Quetzalcoatl salute cannot fully explain the miraculous
transformation. In the earlier part of this passage it is hard to
credit that we are still in Mexico. The language here is not the
language of the earlier part of the novel. It is invested with a quite
new freshness and gentleness. It is like an incident from another
novel; like Mellors showing Connie the newly-hatched pheasant
chicks. It seems that, at the end, Lawrence himself has had too
much of a good thing with Quetzalcoatl and all that, and is ready
to leave the dark gods to the Mexicans, turning to seek for the clue
in human relationships, in love, in togetherness:

> Yet Kate herself had convinced herself of one thing, finally: that the
> clue to all living lay in the vivid blood-relation between man and wo-
> man. A man and a woman in this togetherness were the clue to all
> present living and future possibility. Out of this clue of togetherness
> between a man and a woman, the whole of the new life arose. It was
> the quick of the whole.

After his almost fatal illness of February 1925 Lawrence
turned against Mexico:

> Altogether I think of Mexico with a sort of nausea: . . . really I feel I
> never want to see an Indian or an "aboriginee" or anything in the
> savage line again.

His next novel was to be called *Tenderness.*

Graham Hough
On Lady Chatterley's Lover

Whatever Lawrence happens to be feeling at the moment is apt
to appear to him as a new phase in the history of the world; what
is certainly heralded here is a new phase of Lawrence's development. At one time he thought of calling *Lady Chatterley* "Tenderness," and the word is conspicuous in his comments on the book
in letters. And the tenderness is to be a private and sexual thing,
without any of the political overtones we have become accustomed to in the recent novels.

> I always labour at the same thing—to make the sex-relation
> valid and precious, instead of shameful. . . . Beautiful and tender
> and frail as the naked self is. . . .

> It is a nice and tender phallic novel—not a sex novel in the ordin-
> ary sense of the word. . . . I sincerely believe in restoring the other,
> the phallic consciousness: because it is the source of all real beauty
> and all real gentleness. And those are the two things tenderness and
> beauty, which will save us from horrors. . . .

There is a good deal more, too, about "phallic consciousness"
against "sex consciousness," by which Lawrence means to assert
the primacy of the deepest instinctual forces over the more superficial and personal kinds of attraction more commonly recognised
in the civilized world. There is of course little that is particularly
new in this. It is almost a return to the attitude of *Women in Love,*
and we hear echoes of Birkin's demand for something other than
love and more than it in his relations with Ursula. How far Lawrence advances on this position in these latest works, we must now
inquire.

All the business of private printing, newspaper attacks and
the subsequent *succés de scandale* of *Lady Chatterley* do not
concern us here. Indeed, one would be glad to put all this entirely

From The Dark Sun: A Study of D. H. Lawrence *by Graham Hough.*
The Macmillan Company, 1957. © *Graham Goulder Hough 1956, 1957.*
Reprinted with permission of the Macmillan Company and Gerald Duck-
worth & Co., Ltd.

out of mind in order to see the book as it is in itself and in its continuity with Lawrence's previous work. Nor need we deal in detail with the stages in its growth. Indeed, the evidence is not fully available, and since the story is not closely involved with Lawrence's biography the steps in its composition do not represent a real development, as do those of *Sons and Lovers*. *The Virgin and the Gipsy* looks like an abortive first attempt at *Lady Chatterley,* and *Lady Chatterley* itself was written three times. The earliest version (published in 1944 as *The First Lady Chatterley*) seems only an incomplete realization of the intentions of the final one. The character of the gamekeeper is not very firmly established, and the difference between him and the men of Lady Chatterley's world is shown too much as a mere matter of social class. The second version has not been published, but it has been described, and it seems to be a further step toward the final form. . . .*

The rapid, assured exposition of Connie's background and situation in the early chapters is one of Lawrence's most accomplished pieces of pure straightforward narrative. It is noticeable throughout *Lady Chatterley,* apart from certain special passages to be discussed later, that the writing is exceptionally natural and sure of itself, with no straining after half-realized or unattainable effects. We are at once possessed of Connie's earlier history—of emancipated, pre-war, mildly Bohemian young womanhood. There are experimental love-affairs which never really went deep, the mixing with the young Cambridge group:

> the group that stood for "freedom" and flannel trousers, and flannel shirts open at the neck, and a well-bred sort of emotional anarchy, and a whispering, murmuring sort of voice, and an ultra-sensitive sort of manner.

Clifford comes from another world—an old family, rather isolated and reserved, cut off from the industrial Midlands from which their modern fortune is derived. Connie and he seem to fulfil a need in each other. She gives him a glimpse of a wider life than he has known, and he gives her a companionship that goes beyond sex, where sex indeed seems almost irrelevant. The Chatterleys live utterly apart from the pits and the miners that crowd up to their park gates. The old bond between the classes has gone. Lawrence comments further on this in a valuable essay, "A Propos of *Lady Chatterley's Lover*":

*The second version has since been published under the title of *John Thomas and Lady Jane*. [ed. note]

This, again, is the tragedy of social life to-day. In the old England, the curious blood-connection held the classes together. The squires might be arrogant, violent, bullying and unjust, yet in some ways they were at one with the people, part of the same blood-stream. We feel it in Defoe or Fielding. And then, in the mean Jane Austen, it is gone. . . . So, in *Lady Chatterley's Lover* we have a man, Sir Clifford, who is purely a personality, having lost entirely all connection with his fellow-men and women, except those of usage. All warmth is gone entirely, the hearth is cold, the heart does not humanly exist. He is a pure product of our civilisation, but he is the death the great humanity of the world.

It is an essential part of Lawrence's creed that the social pattern is a reflection of the private sexual pattern. Clifford's isolation from the miners on whom his wealth depends has its root in his isolation from his wife. He wants to say something to Connie about the kind of life that his disability forces upon her, but he cannot bring himself to do it—"he was at once too intimate with her and not intimate enough. He was so very much at one with her, in his mind and hers, but bodily they were non-existent to one another, and neither could bear to drag in the *corpus delicti*." It is tacitly left that he does not mind what steps she takes to remedy the deficiency, as long as he does not positively know about it.

It must inevitably seem here that Lawrence's case is in a fair way to being spoiled by Clifford's physical paralysis. What should be an essential defect of his nature is the result of gross accident, not a part of himself, Lawrence deals with the point in "À Propos of *Lady Chatterley's Lover*"

I have been asked many times if I intentionally made Clifford paralysed, if it is symbolic. And literary friends say, it would have been better to have left him whole and potent, and to have made the woman leave him, nevertheless.

As to whether the "symbolism" is intentional—I don't know. Certainly not in the beginning, when Clifford was created. When I created Clifford and Connie, I had no idea what they were or why they were. They just came, pretty much as they are. But the novel was written, from start to finish, three times. And when I read the first version, I recognised that the lameness of Clifford was symbolic of the paralysis, the deeper emotional or passional paralysis, of most men of his sort or class to-day. I realised that it was perhaps taking an unfair advantage of Connie to paralyse him technically. It made it so much more vulgar of her to leave him. Yet the story came as it did, by itself, so I left it alone. Whether we call it symbolism or not, it is, in the sense of its happening, inevitable.

The real answer is that Lawrence as a novelist, partly by his own fault in using so much of his fiction as the vehicle of doctrine, is often saddled with doctrinaire purposes beyond the actuality. He is not concerned to blame Clifford. As far as the book is doctrinaire its purpose is not to approve one type of character or class against another — it is to show the inevitability of certain profound rhythms of human life. That Clifford cannot help himself, that Connie is a loyal and kind woman, and that there is every moral and humane reason against her doing as she does, makes Lawrence's position all the stronger. And outside the novel, are we not accustomed to consider painful situations, which are no one's fault, and from which no outcome could be happy, as among the most powerful materials of literature?

The slow degeneration of Connie's existence continues.

> Time went on. Whatever happened, nothing happened, because she was so beautifully out of contact. She and Clifford lived in their ideas and his books. She entertained . . . there were always people in the house. Time went on as the clock does, half-past eight instead of half-past seven.

She embarks on a love-affair with one of Clifford's acquaintances, Michaelis, a dramatist. But there is nothing in it, she is as unsatisfied by it as by the utter nothingness before. Clifford's friends are intelligent, in a superficial way, and are even capable of great insight into their situation, though without power to do anything about it. One of them, Tommy Dukes, almost becomes Lawrence's mouthpiece.

> "I wasn't talking about knowledge. . . . I was talking about the mental life. Real knowledge comes out of the whole corpus of the consciousness; out of your belly and your penis as much as out of your brain and mind. The mind can only analyse and rationalise. . . . And if you've got nothing in your life but the mental life then you yourself are a plucked apple, . . . you've fallen off the tree. And then it is a logical necessity to be spiteful, just as it's a natural necessity for a plucked apple to go bad."

And Tommy Dukes does not possess the capacities that he sees to be so essential.

> "I'm not really intelligent, I'm only a mental-lifer. It would be wonderful to be intelligent: then one would be alive in all the parts, mentionable and unmentionable. The penis rouses his head and says: How do you do? to any really intelligent person. Renoir said he

painted his pictures with his penis. . . . he did too, lovely pictures!
I wish I did something with mine. God! when one can only talk!"

Meanwhile Connie meets the gamekeeper Mellors. Clifford
has been entertaining the possibility of her having a son by another
man, to provide an heir for Wragby. They are out in the woods one
day, Clifford in his chair, and Mellors helps to push it up the hill.
Connie is struck by him—quiet, aloof and positive. He is the son
of a collier; went to India and became an officer in the war; his
wife left him while he was away and now he lives alone as a gamekeeper—a deracinated, solitary man. He seems a poor example of
the warmth and intimacy he might be supposed to represent, and
we have here a good illustration of how Lawrence can forget doctrine, become possessed by the genius of fiction—entirely to the
advantage of his work. Mellors is an extremely living and upstand-
ing character, existing in his own right—but he is by no means the
obvious embodiment of what the ideological drift of the book
seems to have been up to now. Indeed, in these opening stages of
Connie's acquaintance with Mellors, all doctrine seems to have
been forgotten, and we have simply the intimate, closely observed
record of the secret growth of a relationship between two people
separated by the barriers of class and condition. Dukes in part
prepares the way for this by maintaining to Connie that mental
intimacy and proper sex relationship are incompatible. She rebels
against the idea, but inwardly she knows he is right. Her next en-
counters with Mellors are mostly disagreeable. He slips into speaking dialect to her, and his manner is coarse and sneering. She
goes to deliver a message at his cottage, accidentally sees him
washing in the yard, and rather to her annoyance is deeply moved
by the sight of his naked torso. This time his manner is perfectly
natural and easy; he is "almost a gentleman," and for a while things
remain in this somewhat enigmatic condition.

There is a fairly long interlude which serves further to develop
Clifford's nature.

Poor Clifford, he was not to blame. His was the greater misfor-
tune. . . . Yet was he not in a way to blame? This lack of warmth,
this lack of the simple, warm, physical contact, was he not to blame
for that? He was never really warm, nor even kind, only thoughtful,
considerate in a well-bred, cold sort of way! But never warm as a man
can be warm to a woman, as even Connie's father could be warm to
her. . . . Clifford was not like that. His whole race was not like that.
They were all inwardly hard and separate. . . . What was the good of
her sacrifice, her devoting her life to Clifford? What was she serving,
after all? A cold spirit of vanity, that had no warm human contacts.

There are more conversations, in which some of Clifford's friends look forward to a future from which all the bother of physical life has been eliminated. Dukes alone stands out, hoping for a resurrection of the body as the only regenerator of a sick civilization. Connie becomes ill, and it is necessary to relieve her of some of the task of tending Clifford. Mrs. Bolton, a nurse from the village, is called in, and Connie begins to breathe more freely.

A good deal is made of Mrs. Bolton. She is one of the vividest minor characters in Lawrence, with a Dickensian sort of vividness that he rarely attempts. Her account of her own life, and her talk about Tevershall, the colliery village, are admirable mimetic writing. Even in the dialogue of *Sons and Lovers* Lawrence does little to imitate the actual speech peculiarities of his characters, but Mrs. Bolton is set before us with less intervention of the author than any other of his personages. When her life is described in *oratio obliqua* it is heavily tinged with her own turns of expression, and when she "talks Tevershall" directly, we have a brilliant piece of sheer mimicry. Imitation of this kind is impossible without a measure of sympathy, and Mrs. Bolton is portrayed with sympathy. She is a vulgar woman, and her part in the plot is an ambiguous one, yet the account of her married life and her husband's death (quoted in part in the Introduction) is one of the few simply moving passages in Lawrence. The sympathy is part of an unwilling tenderness for the country of his boyhood that wells up occasionally in *Lady Chatterley;* but it has another bearing as well. Commonplace, rather commonly power-seeking as she is, by mere virtue of her class Mrs. Bolton avoids the etiolation of the Chatterleys. Her love for her husband has been something real, and her interest in her neighbors, for all its gossipy viciousness, is a kind of human contact. To warmth and humanity on this very low level— so low that he can safely patronize it—Clifford can respond; and he slips more and more under her dominance. The part she plays in the economy of the book, therefore, is to be a counterpoise to Mellors. In a perverse and cross-grained fashion she provides for Sir Clifford some shadow of what the gamekeeper does for Connie. This gives an added symmetry to the plot, which Lawrence is not likely to have cared much about, and, more important, it lessens the burden on Connie when she ultimately decides to leave.

We come now to the heart of the book. Connie becomes increasingly unhappy and dissociated from the life around her. Clifford, on the other hand, finds a new lease of life in managing the mines. It was Mrs. Bolton's suggestion that he should turn his attention to reviving the failing pits, and this cements the alliance

between them. Connie goes frequently to a hut in the woods which
Mellors uses for breeding pheasants. At first he resents her presence and does his best to rebuff her. The place is cool and solitary, and the spring flowers suggest new life, the possibility of
which has long been denied to Connie. The sight of the new-born
pheasant chicks brings this home to her even more acutely.

Mellors appears, and he shows her how to take the chick in
her hands. Suddenly she finds she is crying. He comforts her and
takes her up into the hut. And then—the commentator finds himself against the very barrier that Lawrence is trying to break
through in the rest of the book. How are we to describe what happens? He makes love to her, he sleeps with her, they become
lovers? The hopeless inadequacy of all the standard phrases reveals the difficulty that Lawrence is trying to meet. There is no
adequate language in which the sexual encounter can be even re-
ferred to, still less described; and the new literary problem presented by *Lady Chatterley* is the attempt to find ways of over-
coming this inadequacy.

The first method is simply to describe in detail, and with more
candor than has ever been used before in English letters (or so far
as I know in any other except avowed *erotica*) the immediate
sensations of the lovers:

> Then with a quiver of exquisite pleasure he touched the warm
> soft body, and touched her navel for a moment in a kiss. And he had
> to come in to her at once, to enter the peace on earth of her soft,
> quiescent body. It was the moment of pure peace for him, the entry
> into the body of the woman.
> She lay still, in a kind of sleep, always in a kind of sleep. The
> activity, the orgasm was his, all his; she could strive for herself no
> more. Even the tightness of his arms round her, even the intense
> movement of his body, and the springing of his seed in her, was a kind
> of sleep, from which she did not begin to rouse till he had finished
> and lay softly panting against her breast.

Their first encounter is thus briefly described. The kind of
frantic obscurity in similar attempts in *The Rainbow* is quite absent, the sensations are simply and explicitly presented. So far as
this goes, here and in similar succeeding passages, a new range of
possibilities is opened for the novel. But the experiment is juridical
and social rather than literary. Lawrence is simply describing, in
perfectly familiar terms, something that everyone knows but that
fiction does not commonly describe. He is replacing the novel's
conventional row of asterisks with the words that they conceal.

But there is no new development of language, nor even much of sensibility. All that is needed is the determination to break a taboo. How far is this worth doing, and how far does it succeed? To answer this question we must trace the relations of Connie and Mellors farther.

In this first meeting she is just passive and finds no positive enjoyment. Yet it brings her great peace. She is happy afterward, but he is troubled by foreboding, by the thought of all the complications to follow. We could know all this just as clearly, be just as well aware of what had happened, if we had had the row of asterisks instead of the paragraph of description. But from now on the whole development of the relation of Connie and Mellors depends on the depth and quality of their sexual experience of each other. In many kinds of novel, describing many kinds of relationship, this would be irrelevant; but it is the essence of this particular situation. Therefore if Lawrence is to realize his conception at all fully and openly he must present what is going on as explicitly as possible, must discriminate as fully between different kinds and degrees of sexual fulfilment as the ordinary novelist does between different kinds of sentimental encounter. To put it in the baldest expository terms—Connie gradually comes to experience more direct pleasure in their love-making. There are some failures, more periods of fulfilment, and in the end the experience of complete and abandoned sensual enjoyment, simply for its own sake. Mellors also describes in detail to Connie his earlier married life, and explains to her exactly why he has found happiness with her that he never found in the unsensual loves of his boyhood or with his brutish wife.

Similar material is part of the experience of most men and women. It is obvious that the nature and quality of sexual experience has a powerful influence on character and development. We cannot therefore deny that Lawrence has opened up a wide new territory to the novel by presenting openly what everybody knows in private and what everybody knows to be important. However, other questions remain. How has fiction got on at all in the past, if such a large part of life has been kept behind the curtain? Of course by presenting the subsequent emotional effects of sexual acitivity, its consequences in character and action, without attempting to present the sexual activity itself. It may well be that this is the right procedure. Not only are intimate sexual experiences not commonly talked about in the novel, they are not commonly talked about at all. No one ordinarily puts such experiences into words.* So Lawrence is certainly breaking more than a mere taboo of the printing-house. The instinct for sexual reticence—shame, if one likes to use the pejorative word—though it takes various forms, seems to be deeply ingrained in nearly all cultures. The crucial question, therefore, is whether what is ordinarily never put into words at all can be put into words without altering and deforming the experience. It is a purely empirical question, and I think the unprejudiced answer must be that it can; in the passages I have discussed Lawrence succeeds. The experience of reading this part of the book is less of shock than of recognition. We can say of it what Dr. Johnson said of wit—it is at once natural and new; it is not obvious but on its first production it is acknowledged to be just. Another, and a largely social, question is whether it is necessary or useful to break such a deeply ingrained prohibition. The answer I think is that Lawrence's purpose could not be achieved without it, and that his purpose—to show what he believes to be the place of sensuality in life—is a perfectly legitimate one. But, it must be added, the gain for the novel in general is probably less than might be supposed, and less than has often been claimed. For Lawrence's particular ends it is necessary to describe sexuality in greater detail than has been customary. But his ends are highly individual, the consequence of a quite peculiar development. The freedom to present any aspect of experience is always a gain; but for the purposes of most novelists the traditional method of allowing the detail of sexual life to be inferred from its overt consequences in feeling and action will probably always be more useful.

. . . Connie's progress in sensual satisfaction has already been outlined. It is not an isolated experience; it is accompanied by the experience of warmth, humanity and tenderness as she has never known it before. This expansion of Connie's nature is paralleled by Clifford's development as an industrialist. He makes himself an expert on modern mining methods and soon becomes a considerable power in the colliery world. Connie hates these new interests and the side of Clifford's nature that they bring out. By all ordinary standards this new activity of Clifford's would seem to be an excellent thing; within the context of the book there is a sharp opposition between the expansion of Connie's nature by the warmth of sensual love and the narrowing of Clifford's by the cold lust for power. The hostility between industrial civilization and

*The reader must remember that this excellent essay was written before the recent flood of pornography. [*ed. note*]

sensual tenderness that Ursula had perceived in *The Rainbow* re-appears here in all its old force, and the almost agonized concern with what England had become.

The description of Tevershall . . . modulates into a hopeless lament, seeing only endlessly increasing vistas of squalor stretching into the future.

> England my England! But which is *my* England? The stately homes of England make good photographs, and create the illusion of a connection with the Elizabethans. The handsome old halls are there, from the days of Good Queen Anne and Tom Jones. But smuts fall and blacken on the drab stucco, that has long ceased to be golden. And one by one, like the stately homes, they are abandoned. Now they are being pulled down. As for the cottages of England—there they are—great plasterings of brick dwellings on the hopeless countryside. . . .
>
> What would come after? Connie could not imagine. She could only see the new brick streets spreading into the fields, the new erections rising at the collieries, the new girls in their silk stockings, the new collier lads lounging into the Pally or the Welfare. . . . What next?
>
> Connie always felt there was no next. She wanted to hide her head in the sand: or at least, in the bosom of a living man.

What she sees around her are not living men; but they are all that industrial England has left of humanity.

> So she thought as she was going home, and saw the colliers trailing from the pits, grey-black, distorted, one shoulder higher than the other, slurring their heavy ironshod boots. Underground grey faces, whites of eyes rolling, necks cringing from the pit roof, shoulders out of shape. Men! Men! Alas, in some ways patient and good men. In other ways, non-existent. Something that men *should* have was bred and killed out of them. . . . Supposing the dead in them ever rose up!

The common gibe at Lawrence was that he believed in the regeneration of England by sex. We can begin now to understand what he meant. No society that had preserved a living sense of the full human reality could ever have allowed this degradation to happen. There is no evident cure. One can only hope—a hope not unmingled with fear—that the living sense of human reality may some time rise from the dead. Connie makes her protest against the all-pervading hideousness to Clifford, and is answered, quite rightly from his own premises, with the standard arguments

for industrialism and the managerial society. When she complains
of the hopelessness of the workers' lives and of their own, he
replies that this is just a relic of "swooning and die-away romanti-
cism." And she wonders angrily why Clifford is so wrong, yet she
can never tell him where he is wrong. Of course he is quite right,
by all the assumptions on which modern society is based; and
Connie only dimly knows that if people were rightly related to
each other as individuals such a society would be impossible. . . .

Lawrence has often been criticized for the implied cruelty
of the attitude to Clifford, and for building so much on a relationship that has been an exclusively physical one. I formerly shared
this view, but have now come to believe, within the given context,
that it is wrong. Connie's actions toward him are not excused, for
they are never discussed, in ordinary moral terms. To do so is not
part of the subject of the book. Its subject is the working out of
deep natural laws of human life, which any real morality, according to Lawrence, must take into account. We can then proceed to
criticize Lawrence's whole moral scheme (in the end we must do
so); but it is not legitimate to introduce ordinary social morality
piecemeal into the consideration of an individual work. The relevant questions are whether the work is self-consistent, and whether
its premises are sufficiently consistent with experience to be worth
considering. These have been answered implicitly in all that has
been said up to now. The cruelty in the book is the cruelty of life
rather than that of the author or even of his characters. Lawrence
has weighted the scales against himself by making Clifford an object of pity as well as of legitimate dislike; but no one could maintain that the development from the given circumstances is not
probable in itself or not consistent with the nature of things. It is
true that the relation of Connie and Mellors is an extremely limited
one; they have hardly even held a normal conversation together.
But Lawrence does not suggest or attempt to foresee what their
life together in the future will be like. Still less does he imply that
they married and lived happily ever after. Among the comments
on the book that he quotes in "À Propos of *Lady Chatterley*" is
the following: "Well, one of them was a brainy vamp, and the other
was a sexual moron, so I'm afraid Connie had a poor choice—as
usual!" I do not think that this is quoted quite without the con-
currence of the author. He is remarkably dispassionate toward his
characters. It is the forces working through them that arouse
him most strongly, rather than their personal being; certainly
not the tendency of their actions to move toward a conventional
happy ending.

A more valid criticism is that the relation of Connie and
Mellors is so unlike a normal love relation. Both are deeply injured
and unhappy people: what they find in each other is the almost
desperate satisfaction of desires that have long been cramped and
distorted. And that is not at all like the simple flowering of natural
passion and tenderness which Lawrence wishes to recommend.
Perhaps this is merely to say that the book is more successful as
a novel—for the novel is always about particular people in a particular situation—than as the sexual tract that it is often taken to
be. But it remains true that there is an inconsistency between what
the book actually does and what Lawrence in some of its discursive passages and in the comments in his letters suggests that it
does.

It is also true that here, for the first time, there is no real advance in thought upon earlier work. Up to now, Lawrence's career
as a novelist has been a continual exploration of new territory.
There has been much repetition, but always combined with an
advance. Now for the first time we find him returning upon himself. The message of *Lady Chatterley* is hardly different from that
of *The Rainbow* and *Women in Love;* nor is there any further indication of how it could be applied to existing society. There is
the same belief in a tenderness and passion between individuals
transcending the conscious and personal; the same deep sense that
the right kind of tenderness and passion between individuals must
totally negate the spirit of industrial civilization. But we know no
more than Ursula in her vision of the rainbow how the one is to
overcome the other. The same message, however, is expressed
(apart from the well-defined and separable false notes that we have
indicated) with far greater ease, confidence and maturity of style.
Lady Chatterley is Lawrence's last major work, and speculation
about what would have happened if he had lived longer is an idle
business. The evidence, however, seems to suggest that his spiritual *Wanderjahre* were over, at least for the time. If he had had a
longer period of health and relative stability, it would probably
have been devoted to clarifying and consolidating the insights already gained. We should probably have had nothing completely
new, but a saner and less frenetic statement of much that is already
present in the novels. The Etruscan essays and the little newspaper
articles of his last years all point in this direction. As it is, if after
Lady Chatterley we are to look for one word more, it is to be found
in *The Man Who Died* and in *Last Poems.*

Monroe Engel
The Continuity of Lawrence's Short Novels

Lawrence's short novels are a special and sustained achievement belonging roughly to the last decade of his life. It is of course not clear at precisely what point the long story becomes the short novel, but with *The Fox* (1918–19; revised and lengthened in 1921), not only does Lawrence write a story that is appreciably longer than his earlier stories (about three times the length of "The Prussian Officer," for example), but he establishes certain themes—and, more peculiarly, certain patterns and devices for vivifying these themes—that become generic for his longer stories.

The Fox is written in a markedly objective style verging on irony, or a kind of satire with only the mutest comedy. The elastic fluency of the style also allows direct seriousness, even earnestness. The opening pages describe a peculiar state of disorder suggested by the facts that the two girls in the story are known by their surnames; that March, who had "learned carpentry and joinery at the evening classes in Islington," was "the man about the place"; and that on the farm, nothing prospers: the heifer gets through the fences, and the girls sell the cow—not insignificantly —just before it is to calf, "afraid of the coming event." The fowls are drowsy in the morning, but stay up half the night; and the fox carries them off at will. All in all, the girls "were living on their losses, as Banford said," and they acquired a "low opinion of Nature altogether."

This detailing of disorder is perhaps overdone, labored, and some other elements in the story seem too insisted on also—a kind of heaviness from which the subsequent short novels do not suffer. For March—who is obviously from the first the more restive and savable of the two girls—the fox represents an escape from her present deadening life, an escape conceived in increasingly sexual terms. "Her heart beats to the fox," she is "possessed by him." Then, when the young man appears, he is at once seen in foxy terms. He has "a ruddy, roundish face, with fairish hair, rather long, flattened to his forehead with sweat. His eyes were blue, and very bright and sharp. On his cheeks, on the fresh ruddy skin, were fine, fair hairs, like a down but sharper. It gave him a slightly glistening look." And he is the fabulous fox as well as the natural one, the sly predatory Reynard, for "Having his heavy sack on his shoulders, he stooped, thrusting his head forward. His hat was loose in one hand."

Most of the time, though, the analogy is to the natural fox. The analogy is intentionally overt from the beginning. Lawrence says of the boy that "to March he was the fox"; and once March says to him: "I thought you were the fox." The effect then comes not from a hidden analogy suddenly bursting on the reader's consciousness with the force of discovery, but from the detailed accumulation of the analogy, supported by Lawrence's genius for the description of nature and animals.

The analogy, and March's sexual dream of the fox, are such that we quite accept the remark, late in the story, that March's upper lip lifts "away from her two white, front teeth, with a curious, almost rabbit-look, . . . that halpless fascinated rabbit-look." And accept too the serious weight of sexual implication when she examines the dead fox, and to her hand "his wonderful black glinted brush was full and frictional, wonderful."

The boy's fox-likeness matters—given Lawrence's beliefs—in ways other than simply his vital quickness, or his sexual splendor. There is also "always . . . the same ruddy, self-contained look on his face, as though he were keeping himself to himself." The essential concerns in this story are more nearly simply sexual than in the later ones, but even here this self-contained boy says: "If I marry, I want to feel it's for all my life." And part of his claim to March is that there can be more permanence for her in a relationship with him than in one with Banford. The permanent marriage of two self-contained people is close to Lawrence's ideal.

For of course here as elsewhere, Lawrence is trying to render imaginatively what the relationship between the sexes is and might be, and the contest—between the boy and Banford—for March, is a contest that appears repeatedly, though in various guises, in Lawrence's work: a contest in which the new kind of lover must win the still neutral beloved from the claims of the old kind of love. Banford and March are held together by the old kind of love. Whether that love is also abnormal is largely beside the point. It is not simply that March encases her soft flesh in manly dress for Banford, and shows it in female dress for the boy Henry—though this simple device has enormous and, once more, overt effect in the story. It is rather that March feels responsible for Banford's health and happiness and well-being, and feels safe and sane with her. Sanity and over-responsibility are the marks, in all the short novels, of the old love. It was from these self-destroying feelings that March "wanted the boy to save her."

With Henry—who kills Banford to free March for himself— she feels something else. The story is at its weakest in these final pages, expanded in Lawrence's 1921 revision, which attempt to get at what the nature of the new kind of relationship between man and woman will be. Lawrence, who wished to write social and prescriptive fiction, felt a responsibility to substantiate the better world he preached. A similar impulse and failure can be found in the final act of *Prometheus Unbound*. Each of Lawrence's short novels has this kind of visionary finale, but they become increasingly successful.

The Captain's Doll (1921) is in a similarly objective style, with the author detached even from the proponents of his thesis. But there is less bent of irony this time than of wonder, for *The Captain's Doll* is peculiarly a story about beauty. Again, the meaningful working of the story depends on an overt analogy—between Captain Hepburn and the doll portrait that Hannele makes of him, but doesn't make him into. For this time the analogy is a kind of anti-analogy—the doll is what Captain Hepburn must not become: "any *woman*, today," the Captain says, "no matter *how* much she loves her man—she could start any minute and make a doll of him. And the doll would be her hero; and her hero would be no more than her doll."

All the short novels make heavy use of analogy. This is the only one, however, in which the analogy is to an inanimate object, and the inanimate fixedness of the doll limits its range of usefulness. The use it has, though, is exact and startling, and is at least inherent in the first unseemly appearance of the doll, flourishing head downwards.

Again, as in *The Fox,* the story starts with disordered relationships, and the action concerns the choice a neutral person, Hannele, must make between conventional love and a new kind of relationship. But the choice as posed here is more complicated and rich than in *The Fox.* For one thing, conventional love is given formidable and deeply attractive proponents in Mitchka, the Regierungsrat, and Mrs. Hepburn, who has, in her husband's account of her at least, a quality of out-of-the-world or primitive magic that will recur in the subsequent short novels as a quality reserved for certain adherents of the new order only. Also, the new kind of relationship is suggested more exactly and coherently in *The Captain's Doll* than it was in *The Fox,* and is less simply sexual.

The dramatic acceptability of the doctrine in this story depends on its being given dramatic validity, rather than being merely sermonized as at the end of *The Fox.* It comes too from the substantial impressiveness of Hepburn as a character, and from his and the author's nearly painful sense of the pull and attractions of the old ways, and particularly of the mortal painfulness of beauty (as in the bathing scene in Section xiii). And on the lake, at the very end of the story, we even get a flash of what the life of Hepburn and Hannele may be together, united in this new kind of marriage.

In *The Ladybird* (1921-22), Lawrence told Middleton Murry he had "the quick of a new thing." The "quick" lies chiefly in the character of the Bohemian Count Dionys, who is a resurrected man in a more intellectual, varied, and charming way than Hepburn. Dionys, of course, is purposefully named; but he is the magic Pan, not the vulgar Bacchus.

Again the objective style verges on irony, but this time it is a grave kind of irony, as seen in the opening description of Lady Beveridge. The style is subtle, the exact weight of meaning unfixed. Nothing but such complex fluency of style could make the scenes between Daphne and Count Dionys—and particularly the climactic scene in Count Dionys' bedroom—convincing, and free from any air of the ludicrous.

Again—as in the two previous stories—there is a contest for the neutral soul: the soul of Lady Daphne. But the forces in this contest are not in each case single figures. Lady Beveridge and Basil are a team—the fully civilized or naturally repressed characters, bound to the old civilized kind of selfless love. This is in contrast to Lord Beveridge and Lady Daphne, who are *un*naturally repressed—repressed, that is, in opposition to their own natures. With Lord Beveridge, the repression is nearly final, despite his choleric intransigence and personal integrity. But with Daphne it is not yet final. Even her body cannot accept it, is in disorder, as shown by the tendency to tuberculosis from which she suffers when under stress—a tendency, of course, that Lawrence also had, and which he seems often to have attributed to social causes, to his inability to find a healthy moral atmosphere in which to live. The character who has thrown off civilized repression, the other principal in the contest, is of course Count Dionys.

Perhaps the most remarkable scene in the active contest is

the long debate on love between Count Dionys and Basil, the champion of conventional love, who has told Daphne that his love for her now is a sacrament, and that he considers himself an eager sacrifice to her, and could happily die on her altar. These champions of different attitudes toward love carry on their debate with Daphne sitting between them, finding it "curious that while her sympathy . . . was with the Count, it was her husband whose words she believed to be true." So the schism between her mind, educated to repression, and that other part of her which suffers under this repression, is made dramatically clear. It is an indication of the energy of the ideas and the fluency of the style, that this almost formal debate is always dramatic, never abstracted from the situation, and never tedious—even as is the nobly ludicrous debate between Hepburn and Hannele on the bus in *The Captain's Doll.*

Again animal analogy is important in the story—principally the ladybird analogy from which it gets its title. The ladybird, on the crest of Count Dionys' family, is, he thinks, a descendant of the Egyptian scarab. This leads to a deceptively casual and not quite open exchange:

> "Do you know Fabre?" put in Lord Beveridge. "He suggests that the beetle rolling a little ball of dung before him, in a dry old field, must have suggested to the Egyptians the First Principle that set the globe rolling. And so the scarab became the creative principle—or something like that."
>
> "That the earth is a tiny ball of dry dung is good," said Basil.
>
> "Between the claws of a ladybird," added Daphne.
>
> "That is what it is, to go back to one's origin," said Lady Beveridge.
>
> "Perhaps they meant that it was the principle of decomposition which first set the ball rolling," said the Count.
>
> "The ball would have to be *there* first," said Basil.
>
> "Certainly. But it hadn't started to roll. Then the principle of decomposition started it." The Count smiled as if it were a joke.
>
> "I am no Egyptologist," said Lady Beveridge, "so I can't judge."

The analogy between Count Dionys and this usefully destructive ladybird is admirably clear.

The place of magic—slight and off to one side in *The Captain's Doll,* and to the wrong side at that—is very important in *The Ladybird.* Not the occult theorizing about light and dark—recurrent in so much of Lawrence's fiction—but rather the magic that is conveyed by the songs in the story, the magic of personal power. When Daphne uses the Count's thimble, a German song occurs to her:

> *Wenn ich ein Vöglein wär*
> *Und auch zwei Flüglein hätt'*
> *Flög ich zu dir—*

This is obviously a song of the ladybird, though in her conscious mind Daphne labels it a song of longing for her absent husband. And Daphne is finally brought to the Count—resolving the schism between her conscious and unconscious will—by the "old songs of his childhood" that he sings, an "intense peeping . . . like a witchdraft, . . . a ventriloquist sound or a bat's uncanny peeping, . . . inaudible to any one but herself. . . . It was like a thread which she followed out of the world."

Again the resurrection to a new way is not easy, not a trick, but a painful, chastening separation of the self from the accustomed world and—most painfully, and for Daphne particularly—from its surface beauties. Yet at the end of *The Ladybird,* the reader is convinced that he has glimpsed in Daphne and Dionys some special capacity possessed neither by the other characters in the story, nor by himself.

In *St. Mawr* (1924) the objective style is at times a style of high comedy, and particularly when Mrs. Witt is on scene. Again, of course, the story depends on a central analogy—stressed by the title—between a human being and an animal. But the horse St. Mawr defines Rico not by similarity but by contrast. In this way, the analogy is something like that in *The Captain's Doll.* Once more the analogy is entirely overt, and is suggested or anticipated well before the horse even appears, in a horsey description of Rico in the second paragraph. Rico is all fraudulent play, never the real thing (Mr. Leavis has pointed to the significance of his playing at being an artist). Even his sexuality is bogus. His marriage with Lou is "a marriage . . . without sex"; and so there is brutal irony in the circumstance that he wears a ring, sent him by a female admirer, bearing a "lovely intaglio of Priapus under an apple bough." What Lou requires—and Rico is not at all—is a Dionys, the Pan of the dinner table conversation with the painter Cartwright.

The only men in the story who are at all Pan-like are Phoenix and Lewis, the two grooms, and Phoenix doesn't quite make it either. Lewis, however, is the real thing. He and St. Mawr both avoid physical contact with women because—presumably, and as he says—modern women are incapable of the proper and necessary respect for their husbands. Again, part of the real creative accomplishment of the story is that it can make ideas and notions that we might resist or find absurd out of context, convincing and moving in context. This is particularly true of the long conversation between Lewis and Mrs. Witt during the crosscountry ride they take together to save St. Mawr. The ride culminates with Lewis's refusal of Mrs. Witt's offer of marriage; but before this offer, which ends all exchanges between them, Lewis has shown himself another of the Lawrence characters endowed with otherworldly magic. Mrs. Witt, who in her relations with every other man she ever knew had "conquered his country," feels that Lewis looks "at her as if from out of another country, a country of which he was an inhabitant, and where she had never been." And this magic property is given simpler demonstration by Lewis's naive, stubborn, but only partially credulous talk about falling-stars and ash-tree seeds and the people of the moon. When he sees a falling-star, Lewis thinks to himself: *"There's movement in the sky. The world is going to change again. They're throwing something to us from the distance, and we've got to have it, whether we want it or not."*

St. Mawr is an ambitious story. In the disaster in which St. Mawr is disgraced, he is the figure of unrepressed man ridden by repressed man, Rico. The accident occurs, not fortuitously, when the horse shies at a dead snake. And—supporting the same suggestions—this precipitates for Lou an overwhelming vision of evil.[1]

The magic and visionary qualities emerging through all the preceding short novels, dominate the middle and end of *St. Mawr.* The very end—the description of the deserted mountain ranch in the American Southwest—is a vision of the potential and possibility that Lawrence in his more optimistic thoughts about Amer-

---

[1] It might, incidentally, be interesting to compare Lou's vision on the expedition to the Devil's Chair, and Mrs. Witt's related lassitude toward the end of the story, with the enervating vision of Mrs. Moore in *A Passage to India,* after her visit to the Marabar caves. In a letter to Middleton Murry written just after he had completed *St. Mawr,* Lawrence says: ". . . the *Passage to India* interested me very much . . . the repudiation of our white bunk is genuine, sincere, and pretty thorough, it seems to me. Negative, yes. But King Charles must have his head off. Homage to the headsman."

ica considered it to possess. Lou Witt is not saved here, but is to be brought—possibly—to the condition that precedes any radically new life, a kind of exalted waiting, without sexuality or, really, any connection with other human beings. Lewis and St. Mawr—who has finally found his mate in a long-legged Texas mare: a touch that surely fails to add to the seriousness of the story—drop out before the end, and Phoenix, too, is in effect disposed of. The final pages—marred only at times by Lawrence's preachy vein—give an affecting picture of the beauty and effort of man's attempt to bring order into chaos. And we have here again the Shelleyan attempt to envision with some concreteness the condition abstractly prescribed.

The Man Who Died (1927) is entirely visionary and miraculous. Here the objective style is more formal, to help convey the quality of myth, and again analogy is important. At first Lawrence had called the story "The Escaped Cock"—a title that accentuates the analogy, as do the titles of the other short novels. As usual, the overt import of the analogy requires no expounding.

The theme of the resurrected man (and the Pan-Christ) had occurred in several of the other short novels, in different degrees of importance. Dionys is a resurrected man, coming back to life after being near death, and after considering himself dead and wishing his death. So too is Captain Hepburn in *The Captain's Doll.* In *St. Mawr,* Lou Witt—writing to her mother—says she wishes no more marriages, and understands "why Jesus said: *Noli me tangere.* Touch me not, I am not yet ascended unto the Father. . . . That is all my cry to all the world." And this, of course, is the repeated cry of the man who had died.

It is unnecessary, here, to outline Lawrence's sexual prescriptions. But clearly of great moment in this story are the reverential and respecting wonder between the man and the priestess, and that they know and need to know so little about each other, thus retaining a kind of inviolate personal integrity. Nor is anything like mere sexuality being invoked—not, for example, the slavish sexuality of the slaves. And once more, the extraordinary beauty of the narrative, often gratuitous to its immediate intent, prevents import from becoming anything so meager as doctrine.

These stories have a richness and intricacy—purposeful, and also nearly accidental virtues—that summary cannot suggest. What should be suggested is the achievement not only of form—which often appears to be lacking in the long novels of the same period—but of something very close to formula. There is a bold repetition—often with increasing evidence of intention—of cer-

tain elements, principally: the objective and fluent style; analogy
—generally animal analogy; disordered relationships; the opposition of traditional love and a new kind of relationship between
the sexes, dramatized by a contest between these forces for a
neutral beloved; the use of magic; and the visionary ending, associated with the emergent theme of resurrection, and given final
importance in *The Man Who Died.* Altogether, these short novels
constitute an extraordinary body of imaginatively realized thesis
fiction.

In the short novels, Lawrence puts into practice some of the
objectives he sets himself in the letter to Edward Garnett defend-
ing the early draft of *The Rainbow,* and objecting to the practice
of the great traditional novelists of fitting all their characters into
a moral scheme. This moral scheme is, he says, "whatever the ex-
traordinariness of the characters themselves, dull, old, dead."
For himself, he wants to get away from "the old stable ego of the
character," and make the characters, instead, fall into "some other
rhythmic form, as when one draws a fiddlebow across a fine tray
delicately sanded, the sand takes lines unknown."

For reasons having to do largely with the implications of
length, these more formal principles of characterization may be
more peculiarly suited to the short novel than to the long. In *The
Fox,* the attempt to break the tyranny of the moral scheme is still
flagrant and crude. But in the short novels that follow—particularly beginning with *The Ladybird* and its "quick of a new thing"
—ego in any conventional sense is no longer the spring of action.
Characters act instead in an intricate formal pattern, vivifying and
responding to a central concern. The extremity of Lawrence's
views required highly formal expression to be in any way accept-
able, and the artifice of these short novels is nearly as formal as
ballet or ritual dance.

Kenneth Rexroth
The Poetry of D. H. Lawrence

At the very beginning Lawrence belonged to a different order of being from the literary writers of his day. In 1912 he said: "I worship Christ, I worship Jehovah, I worship Pan, I worship Aphrodite. But I do not worship hands nailed and running with blood upon a cross, nor licentiousness, nor lust. I want them all, all the gods. They are all God. But I must serve in real love. If I take my whole passionate, spiritual and physical love to the woman who in turn loves me, that is how I serve God. Any my hymn and my game of joy is my work. All of which I read in . . ."

Do you know what he read all that in? It makes you wince. He thought he found that in *Georgian Poetry, 1911–1912*, In Lascelles Abercrombie, Wilfred Gibson, John Drinkwater, Rupert Brooke, John Masefield, Walter de la Mare, Gordon Bottomley! What a good man Lawrence must have been. It is easy to understand how painful it was for him to learn what evil really was. It is easy to understand why the learning killed him, slowly and terribly. But he never gave up. He was always hunting for comradeship—in the most unlikely places—Michael Arlen, Peter Warlock, Murry, Mabel Dodge. He never stopped trusting people and hoping. And he went on writing exactly the gospel he announced in 1912, right to the end.

Lawrence thought he was a Georgian, at first. There are people who will tell you that his early poetry was typical Georgian countryside poetry—*Musings in the Hedgerows,* by the Well Dressed Dormouse. It is true that early poems like *The Wild Common, Cherry Robbers,* and the others, bear a certain resemblance to the best Georgian verse. They are rhymed verse in the English language on "subjects taken from nature." Some of the Georgians had a favorite literary convention. They were anti-literary. Lawrence was the real thing. His "hard" rhymes, for instance, "quickkick, rushes-pushes, sheepdip-soft lip, gudgeon-run on." I don't imagine that when Lawrence came to "soft lip" he remembered that bees had always sipped at soft lips and that, as a representative of a new tendency it was up to him to do something about it. I think his mind just moved in regions not covered by the standard associations of standard British rhyme patterns. At the end of his life he was still talking about the old sheep dip, with its steep soft lip of turf, in the village where he was born. Why, once he even rhymed wind and thinned, in the most unaware manner imaginable. That is something that, to the best of my knowledge, has never been done before or since in the British Isles.

The hard metric, contorted and distorted, and generally banged around, doesn't sound made up, either. Compulsion neurotics like Hopkins and querulous old gentlemen like Bridges made quite an art of metrical eccentricity. You turned an iamb into a trochee here, and an anapest into a hard spondee there, and pretty soon you got something that sounded difficult and tortured and intense. I think Lawrence was simply very sensitive to quantity and to the cadenced pulses of verse. In the back of his head was a stock of sundry standard English verse patterns. He started humming a poem, hu hu hum, hum hum, hu hu hum hu, adjusted it as best might be to the remembered accentual patterns, and let it go at that. I don't think he was unconscious of the new qualities which emerged, but I don't think he went about it deliberately, either.

This verse is supposed to be like Hardy's. It is. But there is always something a little synthetic about Hardy's rugged verse. The smooth ones seem more natural, somehow. The full dress, Matthew Arnold sort of sonnet to Leslie Stephen is probably Hardy's best poem. It is a very great poem, but Arnold learned the trick of talking like a highly idealized Anglican archbishop and passed it on to Hardy. That is something nobody could imagine Lawrence ever learning, he just wasn't that kind of an animal.

Hardy could say to himself: "To-day I am going to be a Wiltshire yeoman, sitting on a fallen rock at Stonehenge, writing a poem to my girl on a piece of wrapping paper with the gnawed stub of a pencil," and he could make it very convincing. But Lawrence really was the educated son of a coal miner, sitting under a tree that had once been part of Sherwood Forest, in a village that was rapidly becoming part of a world-wide, disemboweled hell, writing hard, painful poems, to girls who carefully had been taught the art of unlove. It was all real. Love really was a mystery at the navel of the earth, like Stonehenge. The miner really was in contact with a monstrous, seething mystery, the black sun in the earth. There is a vatic quality in Lawrence that is only in Hardy rarely, in a few poems, and in great myths like *Two on a Tower*.

Something breaks out of the Pre-Raphaelite landscape of

Cherry Robbers. That poem isn't like a Victorian imitation of medieval illumination at all. It is more like one of those crude Coptic illuminations, with the Christian content just a faint glaze over the black, bloody "babylonian turbulence" of the Gnostic mystery. I don't know the date of the *Hymn to Priapus,* it seems to lie somewhere between his mother's death and his flight with Frieda, but it is one of the Hardy kind of poems, and it is one of Lawrence's best. It resembles Hardy's *Night of the Dance.* But there is a difference. Hardy is so anxious to be common that he just avoids being commonplace. Lawrence *is* common, he doesn't have to try. He is coming home from a party, through the winter fields, thinking of his dead mother, of the girl he has just had in the barn, of his troubled love life, and suddenly Orion leans down out of the black heaven and touches him on the thigh, and the hair of his head stands up.

Hardy was a major poet. Lawrence was a minor prophet. Like Blake and Yeats, his is the greater tradition. If Hardy ever had a girl in the hay, tipsy on cider, on the night of Boxing Day, he kept quiet about it. He may have thought that it had something to do with "the stream of his life in the darkness deathward set," but he never let on, except indirectly.

Good as they are, there is an incompleteness about the early poems. They are the best poetry written in England at that time, but they are poems of hunger and frustration. Lawrence was looking for completion. He found it later, of course, in Frieda, but he hadn't found it then. The girl he called Miriam wrote a decent, conscientious contribution to his biography. She makes it only too obvious that what he was looking for was not to be found in her. And so the Miriam poems are tortured, and defeated, and lost, as though Lawrence didn't know where he was, which was literally true.

Between Miriam and Frieda lies a body of even more intense and troubled poems. Those to his mother, the dialect poems, and the poems to Helen are in this group. The "mother" poems are amongst his best. They are invaluable as direct perspectives on an extraordinary experience.

From one point of view Lawrence is the last of a special tradition that begins with St. Augustine and passes through Pascal and Baudelaire amongst others, to end finally in himself. There is no convincing evidence for Freud's theory that the Oedipus Complex dates back to some extremely ancient crime in the history of primitive man. There is ample evidence that Western European civilization is specifically the culture of the Oedipus Complex. Before

Augustine there was nothing really like it. There were forerunners
and prototypes and intimations, but there wasn't the real thing.
The *Confessions* introduce a new sickness of the human mind, the
most horrible pandemic and the most lethal ever to afflict man.
Augustine did what silly literary boys in our day boast of doing.
He invented a new derangement. If you make an intense effort
to clear your mind and then read Baudelaire and Catullus together,
the contrast, the new thing in Baudelaire, makes you shudder.
Baudelaire is struggling in a losing battle with a ghost more powerful than armies, more relentless than death. I think it is this demon
which has provided the new thing in Western Man, the insane dynamic which has driven him across the earth to burn and slaughter,
loot and rape.

I believe Lawrence laid that ghost, exorcised that demon,
once for all, by an act of absolute spiritual transvaluation. *Piano,
Silence, The Bride,* and the other poems of that period, should be
read with the tenth chapter of the ninth book of the *Confessions.*
It is the beginning and the end. Augustine was a saint. There are
acts of salvation by which man can raise himself to heaven, but,
say the Japanese, a devil is substituted in his place. Lawrence
drove out the devil, and the man stepped back. Or, as the Hindus
say, with an act of absolute devotion from the worshipper, the
goddess changes her aspect from maleficent to benign.

It is not only that Lawrence opened the gates of personal
salvation for himself in the "mother" poems. He did it in a special
way, in the only way possible, by an intense realization of total
reality, and by the assumption of total responsibility for the reality
and for the realization. Other people have tried parts of this process, but only the whole thing works. This shows itself in these
poems, in their very technique. There, for the first time, he is in
full possession of his faculties. He proceeds only on the basis of
the completely real, the completely motivated, step by step along
the ladder of Blake's "minute particulars." Ivor Richards' *Practical
Criticism* contains a symposium of his students on Lawrence's
Piano. It makes one of the best introductions to Lawrence's poetry
ever written. And one of the qualities of his verse that is revealed
there most clearly is the uncanny, "surreal" accuracy of perception and evaluation. Objectivism is a hollow word beside this complete precision and purposiveness.

From this time on Lawrence never lost contact with the important thing, the totality in the particular, the responsibility of
vision. Harrassed by sickness and betrayal, he may have faltered
in fulfilling that most difficult of all the injunctions of Christ, to

suffer fools gladly. He may have got out of contact with certain kinds of men at certain times. He may have become cross and irritable and sick. But he never lost sight of what really mattered: the blue vein arching over the naked foot, the voices of the fathers singing at the charivari, blending in the winter night, Lady Chatterley putting flowers in Mellors' hair.

The "Helen" poems are strange. (See *A Winter's Tale, Return, Kisses in the Train, Under the Oak, Passing Visit to Helen, Release, Seven Seals.*) They all have a weird, dark atmosphere shot through with spurts of flame, a setting which remained a basic symbolic situation with Lawrence. It is the atmosphere of the pre–War I novel, young troubled love in gaslit London—draughty, dark, and flaring, and full of mysterious movement. Probably the girl's name was not Helen.* Lawrence thought of her as dim, larger than life, a demi-goddess, moving through the smoke of a burning city. For certain Gnostics Helen was the name of the incarnate "female principle," the power of the will, the sheath of the sword, the sacred whore who taught men love. Helen seems to have been the midwife of Lawrence's manhood. At the end, something like her returns in the Persephone of *Bavarian Gentians.* Re-birth. No one leaves adolescence cleanly without a foretaste of death.

Ezra Pound said that the dialect poems were the best thing Lawrence ever wrote. This is just frivolous eccentricity. But they are fine poems, and in them another figure of the myth is carefully drawn. They are poems about Lawrence's father, the coal miner who emerges nightly from the earth with the foliage of the carboniferous jungles on his white body. Lawrence's little dark men, his Gypsies, and Indians, and Hungarians, and Mexicans, and all the rest, are not dark by race, but dark with coal dust. The shadow of forests immeasurably older than man has stained their skins. Augustine was never at peace until he found his father again in the pure mental absolute of Plotinus. Lawrence found his father again in the real man, whose feet went down into the earth. In certain poems where he speaks as a fictional woman, the erotic intensity is embarrassing to those of us who still live in the twilight of the Oedipus Complex. What had been evil in the father image becomes a virtue, the source of the will; deep behind the mother image lies the germ of action, the motile flagellate travelling up the dark hot tube seeking immortality.

The boy watching the miners rise and descend in the yawning maw of the earth in Nottinghamshire grows into the man of forty

*The poems were inspired by Helen Corke, a colleague of Lawrence at the Croydon school. [*ed. note*]

watching the Indians pass in and out of a lodge where an old man is interminably chanting—there is a sense of strangeness, but no estrangement. There is no effort to violate the mystery of paternity because it is known in the blood. Lawrence knew by a sort of sensual perception that every cell of his body bore the marks of the striped Joseph's coat of the paternal sperm. . . .

Some shockingly ill-informed things have been written about Lawrence's relation to psychoanalysis. In the first place, he was not a Freudian. He seems to have read little Freud, not to have understood him any too well, and to have disliked him heartily. In the winter of 1918–1919 he read Jung, apparently for the first time, in English. Presumably this was *The Psychology of the Unconscious.* Jung was very much in the air in those days, as he is again. There was probably a great deal of amateur talk about his ideas amongst Lawrence's friends. But Lawrence does not seem to have had much more to go on, and *The Psychology of the Unconscious* is only the beginning of the system later elaborated by Jung. Nor did he ever become intimate with any of his students. Later Mabel Dodge tried to bring them together by correspondence. The story goes that Jung ignored her letters because they were written in pencil. So much for that.

Lawrence wrote quite a bit on psychoanalysis. There are the two books, *Psychoanalysis and the Unconscious,* a somewhat sketchy popularization of some of Jung's basic concepts, and *Fantasia of the Unconscious,* of which, more in a moment. And then there are the reviews of Trigant Burrow's book, and miscellaneous remarks scattered through correspondence and reviews. This is all of the greatest importance to the understanding of Lawrence. . . .

. . . There is an hallucinatory quality in the images of the poems which precede Frieda which it is interesting to compare with the induced hallucination of H. D. The conflict in H. D. is hidden in herself. It is still there to this day, although her latest prose work has been the journal of a Freudian analysis. Her images are purified of conflict, then the intensity which has been distilled from the sublimation of conflict is applied from the outside. ("Your poetry is not pure, eternal, sublimated," she told Lawrence.) What results is a puzzling hallucination of fact, a contentless mood which seems to reflect something tremendously important but whose mystery always retreats before analysis.

Lawrence's early poems are poems of conflict. The images are always polarized. Antagonisms struggle through the texture. But the struggle is real. The antagonisms are struggling toward the light. The conflict yields to insight, if not to analysis. It is like the propaedeutic symbolism of the dream, as contrasted to the trackless labyrinths of falsification which form the patterns of most waking lives. The hallucination is real, the vision of the interior, personal oracle. Its utterance has meaning, more meaning than ordinary waking reality because the subjective is seen in the objective, emerging from it, the dream from the reality—not dislocated or applied from outside the context.

The poems of *Look! We Have Come Through!* fall into three groups. First there are the structurally more conventional pieces like *Moonrise,* which sounds a little like Masefield's sonnets though it is incomparably finer, and the *Hymn to Priapus,* and the others—they are all probably earlier and have already been discussed. Second, there are the poems of the Rhine Journey, *December Night, New Year's Eve, Coming Awake, History;* erotic epigrams, intense as Mcleager, more wise than Paul the Silentiary. Lawrence was still a young man, and had many great poems to write—but put these beside the few poets who have survived from that day, Sturge Moore, Monro, De La Mare, they look like pygmies. Only Yeats stands up against Lawrence. And last, there are the Whitmanic free verse manifestoes, "explaining" marriage to a people who had forgotten what it was.

With Frieda the sleeper wakes, the man walks free, the "child" of the alchemists is born. Reality is totally valued, and passes beyond the possibility of hallucination. The clarity of purposively realized objectivity is the most supernatural of all visions. Bad poetry always suffers from the same defects: synthetic hallucination and artifice. Invention is not poetry. Invention is defense, the projection of pseudopods out of the ego to ward off the "other." Poetry is vision, the pure act of sensual communion and contemplation.

That is why the poems of Lawrence and Frieda on their Rhine Journey are such great poetry. That is why they are also the greatest imagist poems ever written. Reality streams through the body of Frieda, through everything she touches, every place she steps, valued absolutely, totally, beyond time and place, in the minute particular. The swinging of her breasts as she stoops in the bath, the roses, the deer, the harvesters, the hissing of the glacier water in the steep river—everything stands out lit by a light not of this earth and at the same time completely of this earth, the light of the Holy Sacrament of Marriage, whose source is the wedded body of the bride.

The accuracy of Lawrence's observation haunts the mind

permanently. I have never stood beside a glacier river, at just that relative elevation, and just that pitch, with just that depth of swift water moving over a cobbled bed, without hearing again the specific hiss of Lawrence's Isar. These poems may not be sublimated (whatever Y.M.C.A. evasion that may refer to) but they are certainly pure and eternal.

Again, it is fruitful to compare the Rhine Journey poems with the only other poems of our time which resemble them much, Ford Madox Ford's *Bucksbee*. Ford was writing about something very akin to what Lawrence was, about an aspect of marriage. But he was writing about its impossibility, about how life had bled away its possibility from both him and his girl, and how they had taken, in middle age and in the long Mediterranean drouth, the next best thing—intense erotic friendship. And about how, every once in a while, marriage comes and looks in at the window. The contrast with Lawrence and Frieda, sinking into the twilight in the fuming marsh by the Isar, "where the snake disposes," is pathetic past words.

Ford's *L'Oubi—Temps de Secberesse* and Lawrence's *River Roses* and *Quite Forsaken* are things of a kind and the best of their kind, but like the north and south poles, there is all the difference in the world between them. There is more communion in Frieda's temporary absence than in the closest possible kiss "under the catalpa tree, where the strange birds, driven north by the drouth, cry with their human voices." "Singular birds., with ther portentuous, singular flight and human voices" says Ford. This is the Persephone of *Bavarian Gentians* and the Orphic birds which flutter around the dying who are withdrawing themselves, corpuscle by corpuscle, from communion. Lawrence would come there one day, with the dark blue flowers on the medicine table and Frieda sleeping in a chair beside him, but he was on the other side of the universe then—the early summer of 1912, in the Isartal the show leaving the mountains.

After the Rhine Journey come the poems of struggle for a living adjustment. The ceremonial glory of the sacrament passes from the forefront of consciousness and the period of adjustment to the background of life begins. Every detail of life must be transformed by marriage. This means creative conflict on the most important level.

Sacramental communion is bound by time. Mass does not last forever. Eventually the communicant must leave the altar and digest the wafer, the Body and Blood must enter his own flesh as it moves through the world and struggles with the devil. The problem lies in the sympathetic nervous system, says Lawrence. And it is not easy for two members of a deranged race, in the Twentieth Century, to learn again how to make those webs mesh as they should.

Some of these poems are, in a sense, Frieda's—records of her own interior conquest. It is amazing how much they accomplished, these two. Today, revisiting this battlefield between love and hate that is so carefully mapped in certain of the poems, it is like Gettysburg, a sleepy, pastoral landscape dotted with monuments and graves. Only mained women and frightened men are Suffragettes anymore. Hedda Gabbler is dead, or lurking in the suburbs. We should be grateful to Frieda. It was she who gave the dragon its death blow, and the Animus no longer prowls the polls and bedrooms, seeking whom it may devour.

The Whitmanic poems seem to owe a good deal to *Children of Adam* and *Calamus*. They look like Whitman on the page. But if read aloud with any sort of ear, they don't sound much like him. Whitman flourished in the oratorical context of Nineteenth Century America. He isn't rhetorical in the invidious sense, that is, there is nothing covert or coercive about him. He says what he means, but he says it in the language of that lost art of elocution so popular in his day. There is little of this in Lawrence At this period his long-lined free verse is derived almost entirely from the poetry of the Bible, the Psalms, the song of Deborah, the song of Hezekiah, of Moses, the Benedicite, the Magnificat, the Nunc Dimittis. All the devices of Hebrew poetry are there, and in addition, the peculiar, very civilized, self-conscious "sympathetic" poetry of St. Luke—those poems which have made his the "women's Gospel," and which all good Englishmen must learn in childhood as part of the Morning and Evening Prayer of the Church.
poetry of St. Luke—those poems which have made his the "women's Gospel," and which all good Englishmen must learn in childhood as part of the Morning and Evening Prayer of the Church.

In the volume *Look! We Have Come Through!* Lawrence was just beginning to learn to write free verse. I don't think some of the poems are completely successful. They are diffuse and long-winded. He tries to say too much, and all at the same pitch of intensity; there are no crises, no points of reference. On the whole the most successful is *New Heaven and Earth*. It may not be a perfect object of art, but it is a profound exhortation.

Beyond Holy Matrimony lies the newly valued world of birds, beasts and flowers—a sacramentalized, objective world. "Look, we have come through"—to a transformed world, with a glory around it everywhere like ground lightning. The poems of *Birds, Beasts, and Flowers* have the same supernatural luster that shines through the figures of men and animals and things, busy being part of a new redeemed world, as they are found carved around the mandala of the Blessed Virgin above some cathedral door or on some rose window.

Birds, Beasts, and Flowers is the mature Lawrence, in complete control of his medium, or completely controlled by his demon. He never has any trouble. He can say exactly what he wants to say. Except for the death poems, he would never write better. (And too, after this, he would never be well again.) He seems to have lived in a state of total realization—the will and its power, positive and negative, at maximum charge, and all the universe streaming between them glowing and transformed. The work of art grows in that electric field, is a "function" of it. It is the act of devotion in the worshipper that forces the god to occupy the statue. It is the act of devotion in the sculptor that forces the god to occupy the stone which the artist then pares to his invisible limbs, tailors like cloth. It is never theology in the first; it is never aesthetics or any teachable craft in the second. The craft is the vision and the vision is the craft. . . .

Lawrence's free verse in *Birds, Beasts, and Flowers* is amongst the small best ever written. It can be analyzed, but the paradigms produced by the analysis are worthless. It cannot be explained away, demonstrated in a mathematical sense. Neither, certainly, can any other great poetry; but at least a convincing illusion can be created, and the young can be provided with something to practice. A poem like *Bat,* or *St. Mark,* moves with a stately, gripping sonority through the most complex symphonic evolutions. The music is a pattern of vibration caught from the resonant tone of Lawrence himself. The concerto is not on the page, little spots with flags and tails on a stave, but the living thing, evolving from the flesh of the virtuoso. It is like Gregorian chant or Hindu music, one thing when sung at Solesmes, or in the ruins of Konarak, another when "rendered" by the Progressive Choral Group or at a concert of the Vedanta Society of Los Angeles.

Again, the faults of *Birds, Beasts, and Flowers* are the excess of virtue. Like anyone who knows he has something intensely important to say, Lawrence found it hard to keep from being longwinded. I think a good deal of his over-expansiveness and repetition is due to his methods of composition.

Some poets meditate in stillness and inactivity, as far away as possible from the creative act. We know that Baudelaire and T. S. Eliot, by their own testimony, spent long periods of time quiescent, inert as artists, turning over and over the substance of vision within themselves. Sometimes, as in Baudelaire, this process is extremely painful, a true desert of the soul. Months went by in which the paper and pen were red hot, it was impossible for him to read, his whole personality seemed engulfed in a burning neurasthenia. And then there would come a period of peace, and slowly growing exaltation, and finally the creative act, almost somnambulistic in its completion. Actual composition by this sort of personality tends to be rare, and usually as perfect as talent permits.

Lawrence meditated pen in hand. His contemplation was always active, flowing out in a continuous stream of creativity which he seemed to have been able to open practically every day. He seldom reversed himself, seldom went back to re-work the same manuscript. Instead, he would lay aside a work that dissatisfied him and re-write it all from the beginning. In his poetry he would move about a theme, enveloping it in constantly growing spheres of significance. It is the old antithesis: centrifugal versus centripetal, Parmenides versus Heraclitus. He kept several manuscript books of his verse, and whenever he wanted to publish a collection he would go through them and pick out a poem here and there, the ones he considered had best handled their themes. Behind each poem was usually a group of others devoted to the same material. His selection was always personal, and sometimes it was not very "artistic." *Nettles,* for instance, is a selection of what are, by any standard, the poorer poems of the collections of epigrams printed in *Last Poems.*

There are those who think these epigrams, the ones in *Pansies,* and those in *Last Poems,* aren't art. This opinion is the product of a singular provincialism. It is true that, due to the reasons just mentioned, they aren't all successful, but they belong to a tradition, are members of a species, which has produced some of the greatest poetry. Epigram or maxim, Martial or La Rochefoucauld, the foundations of this tradition are far more stable than those of the neo-metaphysical poetry produced, with seven ambiguities carefully inserted in every line, by unhappy dons between the wars.

Any bright young man can be taught to be artful, It is impossible to teach taste, but you can teach most anybody caution. It is always the lesser artists who are artful, they must learn their trade by rote. They must be careful never to make a false step, never to speak out of a carefully synthesized character. The greatest poetry is nobly disheveled. At least, it never shows the scars of taking care. "Would he had blotted a thousand lines," said Ben Jonson of Shakespeare. Which thousand? Lawrence was always mislaying those manuscript books of poetry and writing around the world for them, just as Cézanne left his paintings in the fields. Not for any stupid reason—that they were not Perfect Works of Art—but simply because he forgot. . . .

As far as I know the poems in the novel *The Plumed Serpent* have never been printed separately. This book is one of the most important (he thought it the most important) Lawrence ever wrote. It has brought forth all sorts of pointless debate. People are always saying: "Well, I have lived in Mexico for years and it *simply* isn't like that." Lawrence was not an idiot. He knew it wasn't. And in the first chapter he gave a very accurate and pitiful picture of the "real" Mexico, sterile, subcolonial, brutal, with the old gods gone, and the church gone, and the revolution a swindle, and nothing left but a squalid imitation of Ashtabula, Ohio. And he knew the other side too, the pasty frigid nymphomaniacs, the deranged women of Europe and America, who consider themselves disciples of Lawrence and prowl the earth seeking Dark Gods to take to bed. He wrote a story which should have destroyed them forever— *None of That.* It should be read with *The Plumed Serpent.*

Every year there is less, but in Lawrence's day there was still something, of the primeval Mexico—at the great feast in Oaxaca, in the life of the peasants in the remote villages, in the Indian communities in the back country. Lawrence did not make any very definite contact with the ancient Mexico but he could see and sense it, and he was fresh from a much less-touched primitive world—that of the Navaho and Pueblo Indians of the Southwest. His materials were not as abundant as they might have been, but they were enough to build a book of ritual, of the possible that would never be, of potentialities that would never emerge. It is a book of ceremonial prophecy, but prophecy uttered in the foreknowledge it would never be fulfilled.

The re-awakening of mystery, the revival of the old Aztec religion, the political "Indianism"—even if it all came true, one knows it would be a fraud, a politician's device, as Indianism is in Latin America today. Lawrence knew that, of course, and so the book is dogged with tragedy. One constantly expects the characters to go out in a blazing Götterdämmerung in some dispute with the police, like a gangster movie. They don't, but maybe it would have been better if they had, for eventually they tire; they seem to become secretly aware that all this gorgeous parading around in primitive millinery, this Mystery, and Fire, and Blood, and Darkness, has been thought up. There is something Western European, British Museum, about it. The protagonist, Kate, submits to her lover's insistent Mystery, but rather out of ennui and loathing of Europe than out of any conviction, and one feels that the book could have no sequel, or only a sequel of disintegration, like *Women in Love.*

Still, in the middle of the book, before the fervor dies out, Lawrence wrote as nearly as he could what be believed should be. If the religion of Cipriano and Ramon is taken as an otherworldly system of values, it is profound and true, and, due to the freshness of its symbols, tremendously exciting. Also, it differs very little from any other religion that has maintained its contacts with its sources. Ramon and Cipriano short-circuit themselves where Christianity was short-circuited by Constantine, in the desire to have both worlds, to found a political religion—a Church. That, if any, is the "message" of the book.

The mystery survives in the poems, just as the sacraments survived Constantine. They are not the greatest poems Lawrence ever wrote, but they are amongst the most explicit. This is Lawrence's religion. Wherever he found it he is now in complete possession of a kind of orthodoxy, the orthodoxy of the heterodox— the symbolic world of the Gnostics, the Occultists, Tantrism, Jung. In a sense they are failures, these poems, in the way that the Indian songs published by the United States Bureau of Ethnology are not failures. But, again, that is the message of the book. Finally you discover that you cannot make up paganism. What you make up is a cult. There is nothing primitive about Gnosticism, anymore than there is anything primitive about Theosophy. It is the creation of over-civilized Hellenistic intellectuals. Tantrism too grew up in India, in Buddhism and Hinduism, when civilization was exhausting itself. Jung comes, with Lawrence, at the end of the career of Western European Man. Lawrence, after all, was a contemporary of Niels Bohr and Picasso. And so his poems are mystical poems—and the Aztecs were not mystics, they were just Aztecs. This doesn't invalidate the poems. They have very little to do with ancient or modern Mexico but they do express, very well, the personal religion of D. H. Lawrence. They may be full of "occult lore," but behind the machinery is an intense, direct, personal, mystical apprehension of reality.

In the last hours Lawrence seems to have lived in a state of suspended animation, removed from the earth, floating, transfigured by the onset of death. Poems like *Andraitix—Pomegranate*

Flowers have an abstracted, disinterested intensity, as though they were written by a being from another planet. Others are short mystical apothegms. There is no millinery anymore, no occultism, they differ only in their modern idiom from any and all of the great mystics. And finally there are the two death poems, *Bavarian Gentians* and *The Ship of Death*. Each was written over several times. There exists a variant which can be taken as a final, or prefinal, version of *Bavarian Gentians,* but both are clusters of poems rather than finished products.

The Ship of Death material alone would make a small book of meditations, a contemporary *Holy Dying*. It is curious to think that once such a book would have been a favorite gift for the hopelessly ill. Today people die in hospitals, badgered by nurses, stupefied with barbiturates. This is not an age in which a "good death" is a desired end of life.

All men have to die, and one would think a sane man would want to take that fact into account, at least a little. But our whole civilization is a conspiracy to pretend that it isn't going to happen—and this, in an age when death has become more horrible, more senseless, less at the will of the individual than ever before. Modern man is terribly afraid of sex, of pain, of evil, of death. Today childbirth, the ultimate orgiastic experience, has been reduced to a meaningless dream; dentists insist on injecting novocaine before they clean your teeth; the agonies of life have retreated to the source of life. Men and women torture each other to death in the bedroom, just as the dying dinosaurs gnawed each other as they copulated in the chilling marshes. Anything but the facts of life. Today you can take a doctor's degree in medicine or engineering and never learn how to have intercourse with a woman or repair a car. Human self-alienation, Marx called it. He said that was all that was really wrong with capitalism. "Let us live and lie reclined" in a jet-propelled, streamlined, air-cooled, lucite incubator. When we show signs of waking, another cocktail instead of the Wine of God. When we try to break out, flagellation instead of Holy Matrimony, psychoanalysis instead of Penance. When the machinery runs down, morphine for Extreme Unction.

In a world where death had become a nasty, pervasive secret like defecation or masturbation, Lawrence re-instated it in all its grandeur—the oldest and most powerful of the gods. The *Ship of Death* poems have an exaltation, a nobility, a steadiness, an insouciance, which is not only not of this time but which is rare in any time. It doesn't matter who: Jeremy Taylor, the Orphic Hymns, the ancient Egyptians—nobody said it better. And there is

one aspect of *The Ship of Death* which is unique. Lawrence did
not try to mislead himself with false promises, imaginary guaran-
tees. Death is the absolute, unbreakable mystery. Communion and
oblivion, sex and death, the mystery can be revealed—but it can be
revealed only as totally inexplicable. Lawrence never succumbed
to the temptation to try to do more. He succeeded in what he did
do.

Dan Jacobson
D. H. Lawrence and Modern Society

Any discussion of the social and political thought of D. H. Lawrence is bound to be largely a discussion of his hatred of modern
society. None of the greatest twentieth-century writers in English
have been at all kindly disposed toward industrialism and the
political and cultural developments which they believed inevitably
accompanied it: democracy, science, urbanism, liberalism, religious scepticism, egalitarianism, the spread of the mass entertain-
ments. But of all the haters of the modern world Lawrence was the
most intense and unremitting; in comparison with his hostility
that of such different figures as W. B. Yeats and T. S. Eliot can
appear almost mild, and even at times self-satisfied. For one thing,
both Yeats and Eliot were eager to find some kind of institutional
framework or support for their contempt of modern society: in
the Anglican church in Eliot's case, in an idea of country-house
civilization in that of Yeats, in right-wing political movements in
the case of them both. For this reason they lay themselves open to
the charge that in rejecting democracy and industrialism they were
in fact seeking to protect the interests of some special group within
the existing society. Nothing of the kind is true of Lawrence; it can
be said that the only interests he was trying to preserve were his
own; and as a result of his rejection has a quality of purity and radi-
calism lacking in the others.

In the period beginning, say, with the last quarter of *The Rainbow* and ending with *The Plumed Serpent,* Lawrence worked out a
theory of human nature and society which is more persistently and
consistently argued out from book to book and essay to essay than
has generally been allowed. But it is not an easy matter for the
reader to decide just what Lawrence's "doctrine" is and how it
should best be taken. Though he committed himself far more than
most other novelists to the development of this theories in discursive works like *Psychoanalysis and the Unconscious* and
Studies in Classic American Literature, Lawrence was primarily

From Journal of Contemporary History, *April 1967. Copyright © 1967*
Journal of Contemporary History. *Reprinted by permission of Russell &
Volkening, Inc., New York.*

an artist, and if we are to respond adequately to his work we must respond to it as a whole: above all, we must try to respond to the imaginative veracity of the fictional world he created, or failed to create, in each of his novels. Paradoxical though it may seem, my own conviction is that what is merely self-willed or self-serving or unexamined in Lawrence's theories is likely to betray itself by arbitrariness and incoherence in the fiction—*not* because I think of the fiction as a mere animation of the theory, but because that is precisely what the fiction becomes when the theory takes command of it. To know how much public, salutary truth there is in what Lawrence has to tell us, and how much private paranoia and special pleading, we have to decide whether his characters, scenes, and dramatic actions bear out in the fulness of their imagined life the conclusions which are being drawn from them, or whether we feel the conclusions to be *a priori,* thrust upon the work, a distortion of it.

There is another difficulty in discussing Lawrence's social or political thought which should be mentioned here; and that is that the very essence of his doctrine is the denial that one could talk constructively about society and the political and economic order without invoking ultimate sanctions; without, in other words, talking about the religious needs of the individual and the community. For Lawrence, to think about men in relation with one another as citizens, or as producers or consumers, was necessarily to think about the relationship of each with his innermost self and with the force or forces which govern the universe. Indeed, one of the main reasons why he detested modern life so profoundly was because he believed it was driven by the impulse to assert the self-sufficiency of man, his independence from the natural order. The modern world, as he saw it, encouraged men to believe that they could find fulfilment as producers and consumers of material goods, as members of competing political parties or nation-states, as manipulators of yet more and more powerful machines, instead of as creatures whose ultimate allegiance should always be to non-human forces outside themselves and greater than themselves.

In its assertion that the industrialization of society has brought about a catastrophic uprooting of man from nature (and hence from his own true nature), Lawrence's critique of modern life can be assimilated without much strain into the tradition of protest against industrialism which dominated so much nineteenth-century writing in England: one can see Lawrence easily enough in the line in which belonged writers like Coleridge, Dickens (of *Hard Times* and *Little Dorrit*), Carlyle, Ruskin, Matthew Arnold, and William Morris. To them all, the coming of the machine meant the mechanization of man; a fostering of the spirit of calculation and possessiveness and an impoverishment of human warmth and individuality; a disruption of the spirit of community; an irrevocable loss of some of the most valuable traditions of the race; an abridgement or destruction of its religious instincts.

All this, as I say, is a note which recurs throughout nineteenth-century literature; and, with some differences, it sounds loudly enough in the literature of the first half of the succeeding century. However, what Lawrence added to the chorus is entirely individual. Many of the names mentioned above would have drawn back in dismay at Lawrence's fierce assertion that much that had always been considered finest and most valuable in the history of Western civilization found its logical culmination in the black horrors of industrialization. Those writers would have been as dismayed as most humanists and humanitarians are today when they realize that what frequently roused Lawrence's wrath were just those social and moral ambitions which are generally regarded as compensations for the disorders and dangers of technological development. He was inclined to see modern benevolence as evil, the modern passion for social justice as misdirected, the modern diffusion of physical comfort and security as a corruption, the notion of the sanctity of the individual "personality" as a tyranny and disease. It is important to notice that it was not the failure (in so many places, at so many times) of the contemporary society to achieve its own ambitions that infuriated him, as we can perhaps say about someone like Dickens: it was the attempt itself.

For example:

> The ideal of love, the ideal that it is better to give than to receive, the ideal of liberty, the ideal of the brotherhood of man, the ideal of the sanctity of human life, the ideal of what we call goodness, charity, benevolence, public spiritedness, the ideal of sacrifice for a cause, the ideal of unity and unanimity—all the lot—all the whole beehive of ideals—has all got the modern bee-disease, and gone putrid, stinking. And when the ideal is dead and putrid, the logical sequence is only stink. Which, for me, is the truth concerning the ideal of good, peaceful, loving humanity and its logical sequence in Socialism and equality, equal opportunity or whatever you like. By this time he stinketh—and I'm sorry for any Christus who brings him to life again, to stink livingly for another thirty years: the beastly Lazarus of our idealism.

The passage comes from *Aaron's Rod,* from a speech by Lilly, who is plainly the voice and presence of Lawrence in the novel.

Any reader of Lawrence will know that it can be paralleled by
scores of similar passages from the works which immediately
preceded and followed *Aaron's Rod,* and from the letters of the
period. One way of meeting this strain in Lawrence's work is simply to call him a fascist, as many people have done, or to say, with
C. P. Snow, that he displays "imbecile anti-social feeling"—and
have done with it. But it seems to me more useful to say that we
can dissent from outbursts such as these and yet acknowledge
that behind them, as the novels show, there lies a great deal of
intense thought and painful experience, which we owe it to ourselves to try to understand and from which we may have something
to learn.

Lawrence's theory of the individual psyche, on which his theory
of society depends, can be summarized crudely enough as follows:
Within each individual there is a "dark self" (or "blood being," or
"blood consciousness" or "active unconsciousness") which exists
independently of, and anterior to, "the ordinary mental consciousness" (or "white self" or "personality" or "social ego" or "mental-
subjective self"). When the psyche is healthy, the dark self, which
is the true source of the passions, the true center of response to the
outside world, has primacy and power over the mental consciousness, which should properly do no more than transmute the "creative flux" of life into what Lawrence called the "shorthand" of
ideas, abstractions, principles, ideals.

However, when the relationship of forces within the individual
is disturbed, the mental consciousness, with its ideas and ideals,
can usurp the primacy which should belong to the dark self; it
repudiates the life of the body and the senses, and then seeks to
impose upon the rest of the person the fixed, static abstractions
which are all that it knows, all that it contains. Instead of being
open and receptive before the world, aware always of the "other-
ness" of the world to himself, the man becomes a creature of his
own fixed will, self-enclosed, self-referring, insentient; he becomes an automatism, a system, a machine.

I do not wish to press too heavily on the last few words; but it
is certainly true that in the Lawrencean scheme of things the af-
finity between the "machine" of the runaway mental consciousness
and the machines of the industrial world is more than metaphor-
ical. An individual who has degenerated in this particular way,
who has turned himself into a machine, inevitably sees the natural
world and human society as fields for the exercise of his will, instead of as the "spontaneous-creative" flux they really are. But

once the industrial system exists "outside" in the world, anyway, it in turn forces into its own shape the psyches of those who live within it. The community ceases to exist, and becomes instead an agglomeration of so many enclosed egos, each convinced of its own self-importance and all alike submitting willingly, greedily, competitively, to material measurements of welfare and quality.

This state, Lawrence insists, is what we have been brought to by "the human idealism which governs us now so ruthlessly and so vilely"; and he sees the liberal, the capitalist, the communist and the Christian all committed equally to it. "What tyranny," he asks, "is so hideous as that of an *automatically ideal humanity?*" (My italics.)

If we set aside the industrial or mechanical metaphor which Lawrence uses so freely, I think the similarity between some of what he is saying and the theory of the psyche which Freud adumbrated is striking—though Lawrence himself always denied strenuously that his conception of the "true unconsciousness" had anything in common with "the cave . . . of unspeakable horrors" that Freud had spoken of. That may be so. But Lawrence's description of the mental consciousness or will and of the havoc it can wreak on the psyche must remind us of the Freudian picture of the superego: punitive, determined, involuntary in its operations. The resemblance to the Freudian superego is made all the more pronounced by the fact that Lawrence believed much the most powerful of the abstractions which had become fixed into a series of murderous injunctions from the mental consciousness were those drawn from centuries of propagation of Christianity, and those secular gospels of love and social welfare which were derived in one form or another from Christianity. (It is not accidental that the image of Christ is quite specifically brought into the diatribe from *Aaron's Rod* quoted above.) It was against the gospel of love that he reacted most fiercely: against love in its religious forms; love in the ordinary sexual meaning of the word; and love in its modern material manifestations, in what he called "the industrial-lovey-dovey-darling-take-me-to-mamma state of things."

Now it does seem odd indeed that a writer in the twenties of this century, a few years after the end of the First World War and the Russian revolution, a few years before the rise of Hitler to power, and in the middle of the economic crises which racked that period, should condemn his society for being "lovey-dovey," rather than for being cruel, bloodthirsty, rapacious, and hysterical. But in fact, Lawrence was ready to blame the lovey-dovey idealists of every political hue for being bloodthirsty as well. Beneath the tyranny of an insenate "automatic idealism," the raped and despoiled dark self suffered and sought its revenge; so that those who claimed to uphold the conscious ideals of their society were filled with a secret, desperate craving for destruction and anarchy, and had done and would continue to do their utmost to bring the world to ruin.

Do the novels of the particular period of which I am speaking bear out this diagnosis? Imaginatively, in the fullness of their artistic life? Our answer must be: not entirely, not as Lawrence would have wished them to. I shall give just two illustrations of what I have in mind, the one from *Women in Love* and the other from *Kangaroo*. I emphasize that while the examples are chosen from among many others which could be offered, at the same time I am following only a single track through novels which are far more extensive than I can hope to indicate.

In *Women in Love* the character who carries the burden of embodying for us the destructive nihilism of the modern world, with its surface kindliness and productiveness and its inner "malignity," is Gerald Crich, mine-owner and lover of Gudrun Brangwen. Ranged against him, in admiration, sympathy, and despair, is Rupert Birkin, inspector of schools and lover of Ursula Brangwen. Birkin, everyone agrees, is Lawrence's spokesman in the novel; it is he who makes the most trenchant analyses of the sickness of the soul which assails Gerald. But of the two men it is Birkin who gives utterance repeatedly to a sheer hatred of humankind, which, in effect, goes unreproved in the novel; one can almost say that it is hardly remarked on, either by Birkin himself or by any of the other characters. This is all the more striking because one of the main dramatic functions of Ursula is to bring Birkin down to earth when he gets carried away, to speak up for commonsense in the face of his tirades. She does it again and again; but not when Birkin expresses his passionate longing to see the human race wiped out. Then, and then only, Ursula agrees with him, or *regretfully* reminds him that that consummation is really rather too much to hope for. (See Chapter XI, "An Island," in particular.) In a way, Ursula's defection here strikes us as even more of an artistic self-betrayal by Lawrence than Birkin's tirade itself.

My point is that the case against Gerald, and against the system he upholds, is radically damaged by the force of repudiation and misanthropy which we feel to be operating in so many passages throughout the book. The malignity which is so insistently imputed to Gerald becomes for us too often, though not invariably, a further example of the malignity of his creator. *Women in Love* is by any standards a great novel, as original in its approach to character and theme as in its vocabulary of the emotions; I have given only a very partial account of its treatment of Gerald. Yet, being the first novel in which Lawrence's social theories receive full-length dramatic presentment, it is also the first to rouse the suspicion that he is incapable of accounting for his hatred of "love" and of "the peace and production stunt"; that his hatred springs from motives he does not understand and is unable to make effective in his art.

Kangaroo is, of course, a much looser, less arduous, less important work than *Women in Love;* Lawrence can almost be said to have let the book write itself. In large part it is simply an account, which shows Lawrence at his wittiest, most relaxed and penetrating, of his and Frieda's experience in Australia; it contains also the famous chapter describing Lawrence's treatment at the hands of the English authorities during the war. But with all this, *Kangaroo* is also a sustained attempt by Lawrence to imagine himself taking part in political action; to imagine himself joining a political movement, and so curing the ache of separation from his fellow-men which he felt so acutely.

The political party to which Richard Lovat Somers, Lawrence's *alter ego,* is attracted can only be called fascist in character. Made up for the most part of ex-servicemen, organized in secret cells, with the strictest hierarchy of command, functioning through oaths of total obedience, insisting that it stands "above" or "apart from" all the political parties, the Diggers movement which Lawrence created obviously owed a great deal to what Lawrence had seen in post-war Europe, in Italy and Germany in particular. The members of the movement go in for military training and revolver practice; they plan to take advantage of any crisis to seize power and to impose upon the country what the leader of the movement, Kangaroo, openly speaks of as a dictatorship.

Now it is clear from the shape and form of the book (not to speak of the shape and form of Lawrence's life) that Somers will not stay in Australia; that he will have to break with the Diggers and leave. So Lawrence has to arrange for Somers to have a personal rupture with Kangaroo. At this point, in order to give Somers a reason for the break which will be emotionally convincing to Lawrence himself, a complete nonsense is made of the entire political aspect of the book. The Diggers movement is dedicated

to violence and authoritarianism; but when Somers repudiates
its leader he does so because Kangaroo has suddenly and absurdly
begun to preach the gospel of love.

> The love of man for wife and children, the love of man for man,
> so that each would lay down his life for the other, then the love of
> man for beauty, for truth, for the right. . . . Destroy no love. Only
> open the field for further love.

With speeches of that kind, Kangaroo disgusts Somers and
his creator, and thereby sets them free from the need to feel the
remotest allegiance to him. One cannot help feeling that if the
Diggers had heard Kangaroo making such speeches (and after all
their revolver practice, too!) they would have been quite as dis-
gusted with him as Somers—and almost as surprised as the reader.
The direction of the *idées fixes* which these two examples
fairly illustrate makes logical enough Lawrence's development
toward that notorious book, *The Plumed Serpent.* The story of
the imagined rebirth in Mexico of the old, bloodthirsty Aztec
religion, with its ritual murders and its sacerdotal notions of "leadership," represents Lawrence's most frenzied rejection of the
gospel of love in its social, sexual, and religious forms. Despite
a brilliant opening, it is also Lawrence's worst novel, by far; the
one which is least the product of his artistic sensibility and most
that of a bullying, obsessed will which cannot afford to become
aware of the true character of its own compulsions. That fixity of
will, by the way, reveals itself not only in the cruel or vindictive
episodes of *The Plumed Serpent* and various other works, but also
in many of their supposedly hopeful passages, their apocalyptic
or millenarian predictions, their vatic assertions that a totally
new and better world is imminent, another finer race of humans
is about to be born.

Lawrence has been the subject of so much amateur and profes-
sional psycho-analysis that I have no inclination to guess just why,
when he lost his poise as a man and an artist, he should have succumbed to the particular involuntary, hysterical patterns of reaction whose outlines I have tried to suggest above. But that he
did so, and that these reactions always threatened the value and
disinterestedness of his social views seems to me undeniable.
Some people would defend this aspect of Lawrence's work by
saying that all we can ask of any artist is that he should "embody"
the forces of his age and give them tongue—which Lawrence

surely to some extent did in the murderous dreams to be found in *Women in Love, Kangaroo,* and *The Plumed Serpent.* My objection to this view is that the artist should not only embody these forces, but that his art should embody an understanding of them too; or at least be the record of his striving toward it. I have tried to indicate how damaging to Lawrence's art could be the results of his intermittent failures to make such an effort.

However, the nature of creativity is such that we should not really be surprised that the neurasthenic malice and fear which sometimes possessed Lawrence should have been intimately connected with a sense of the actualities and possibilities of life which elsewhere expressed itself in an achievement ranking among the very greatest in English literature. Through the circumstances of his birth, upbringing, and later wanderings, Lawrence was compelled to confront, in so many different parts of the world, the social and material revolutions of his time, to grasp the vast scope of the transformations he was witnessing, and to try to divine their inner meanings—the human drives and potentialities they had emerged from, the effects they were likely to have on individual and group consciousness.

I have spoken of Lawrence as a thoroughgoing revolutionary and radical, and so he was in any ordinary political or social meaning of the words. But it does not seem to me a contradiction to go on to say that the best of Lawrence's work represents a passionate plea for, a striving towards, and often enough an attainment of, a condition of *balance.* This condition, of which he spoke explicitly, his favorite word for it being "polarity," is of the greatest importance in bringing together his psychological speculations, his social theories, his view of the relationship between the sexes, and his view of the relationship which should exist between men and nature. In the successful sections of all the novels I have discussed, in almost the whole of *The Rainbow,* in much of *The Lost Girl,* in the extraordinary variety and richness of the best of his *nouvelles,* stories, and poems, the idea of balance is much more than a concept or theoretical construct; it is a state which the art itself attains, and whose value we appreciate all the more keenly because we see, in the narrative, dramatic and poetic development of each work, how difficult it is to achieve and how easily it can be disrupted.[1] The swaying, delicate nature of the

---

[1] *Lady Chatterley's Lover* seems to me a brave, touching, and unsuccessful attempt to escape from the emotional and artistic dead-end reached in *The Plumed Serpent.*

equilibrium, the fact that it is always unstable, is precisely the sign of its life; and no threat to it is greater than the attempt to make it fixed, firm, and permanent. No matter how high-minded, generous, or compassionate the ostensible motives of such an attempt might be, Lawrence again and again shows us, its effect must always be deathly.

Though the concept of balance has its real imaginative vindication in the art, its importance is patent enough in any discussion of Lawrence's theories as such. We can see it most obviously, perhaps, in what I have called his theory of the psyche, in his insight into the dangers of "abstract idealism," which I have compared with Freud's. ("Civilized society exacts good conduct," Freud wrote during the First World War, at the time when Lawrence was entering the most tortured period of his creative life, "and does not trouble itself with the impulses underlying it. . . . Encouraged by its own success, society forces its members into an ever greater estrangement from their instinctual dispositions.") That Lawrence was sometimes wrong in his diagnosis of what elements in society were most truly estranged from themselves, that his work occasionally is itself flawed by the functioning of a hypertrophied will, is less important than his perception that estrangement of this kind was an ever-present danger, and one which was likely to grow more and more intense as civilizations increased in technological complexity. Indeed, it is a tribute of a kind to Lawrence's insights that they can be turned so effectively against his own work, when the weakness of the work invites one to do so. He could not see that he himself was making an "abstract idealism" out of his repudiation of the ethics of peace of production; nor how hideous the consequences of such a repudiation could be when it was actually turned into a program, a policy, an ethic of war and destruction. But his failure in this regard does not mean we can afford to be indifferent to the other psychic rigidities and inanitions, and their intellectual and political consequences, which he was so often able to diagnose so accurately.

The idea of balance or polarity necessarily implies forces in relation to one another; and it is true of Lawrence's development and illustration of the concept that it was essentially dynamic, it always engaged his sense of the interdependence of all aspects of life with one another. But if he was profoundly aware of the "oneness" of life, it was not at the cost of forgetting that consciousness exists only in individuals. It was partly because of his acute feeling for the individuality of consciousness that he so much hated the thought of "merging," whether in the relationship between the sexes or in what he felt to be the indiscriminate, engulfing demands and processes of the industrial system; at the same time, he believed that men without a sense of community with one another were less than complete, as were men and women who denied their need for one another or who tried to use that need for their own consciously determined ends. He insisted that nature was not "ours" to exploit or despoil as we willed; and what was true of the nature external to us was true also of that with which we were born.

The last thing I would wish to suggest is that the great Lawrence was "really" a humanitarian who now and again went astray or who laid himself open to misunderstanding. Far from it; he was nothing of the kind. In fact, one of the things that people of humane instincts can learn from him is that it is possible to have a deep sense of responsibility about human life without therefore feeling obliged to make the diminution of pain the primary task of all social thought and action. Lawrence's preoccupations were of quite another, though hardly less important, kind. He wanted to make life not easier, but more meaningful. Today, when the material conditions of life in the developed countries are much easier for many more people than they used to be, and when at the same time the whole human enterprise is threatened in a way it never has been before, we have to acknowledge the continuing relevance of the questions he attempted to raise, the warnings he tried to sound, the alternatives he tried to explore.

It is fairly easy to make a program of action out of the worst in Lawrence's work, impossible to make one out of his strengths. The best of his work has the power to present to us, with an extraordinary imaginative intensity, those human needs and aspirations which all our programs should ultimately be intended to serve.

Bibliography

LAWRENCE'S WORKS

The arrangement is by genre. There is also a list of biographical and critical works that will provide further information about Lawrence's works and the scholarship devoted to them.

Dates of original publication are given in parentheses. The date of the writing is indicated by "C." For convenience, details are given of some modern editions; for full details concerning first editions, the reader should consult Warren Roberts, *A Bibliography of D. H. Lawrence.*

Novels

The White Peacock (1911). C. 1906–10. Everyman's Library, Heinemann, Penguin, Southern Illinois University Press.
The Trespasser (1912). C. 1910–12. Heinemann, Penguin.
Sons and Lovers (1913) C. 1910–13. Heinemann, Penguin, Compass, Harper, Modern Library.
The Rainbow (1915). C. 1913–15. Heinemann, Penguin, Compass.
Women in Love (1920). C. 1915–17. Heinemann, Penguin, Compass, Modern Library.
The Lost Girl (1920). C. 1913–1920. Heinemann, Penguin.
Aaron's Rod (1922). C. 1917–21. Heinemann, Penguin, Compass.
Kangaroo (1923). C. 1922–23. Heinemann, Penguin, Compass.
The Boy in the Bush (with M. L. Skinner, 1924). C. 1923. Penguin.
The Plumed Serpent (1926). C. 1923–25. Heinemann, Penguin, Vintage.
Lady Chatterley's Lover (1928) Three versions: (1) C. 1926, *The First Lady Chatterley,* Dial Press, New York, 1944; (2) C. 1926–27, *John Thomas and Lady Jane* (1972). Heinemann, Viking; (3) C. 1927–28, unexpurgated version, Signet, Penguin, Pyramid, Grove, New American Library, others.

Short Novels and Tales

The Short Novels (1956). Heinemann, Compass.* In two volumes: I—*Love Among the Haystacks, The Ladybird, The Fox, The Captain's Doll;* II—*St. Mawr, The Virgin and the Gypsy, The Man Who Died.*

*The Compass edition of the short novels differs from the English edition.

The Complete Short Stories (1955). Heinemann, Compass. In three volumes. Not included are "Mr. Noon," "A Prelude," "Once," "The Thimble," and "The Mortal Coil," which appear in *Phoenix II.*

Travel Books

Twilight in Italy (1916). Heinemann, Penguin, Compass.
Sea and Sardinia (1921). Heinemann, Compass.
Mornings in Mexico (1927). Heinemann, Penguin (with *Etruscan Places*).
Etruscan Places (1932). Heinemann, Penguin, Compass.

Theoretical Works

The Crown (1915)—in *Phoenix II.*
Psychoanalysis and the Unconscious (1921). Heinemann and Compass (with *Fantasia*).
Fantasia of the Unconscious (1922). Heinemann, Compass.
Reflections on the Death of a Porcupine (1925)—in *Phoenix II.*
Apocalypse (1931). Compass, Albatross.

Poetry

The Complete Poems (1964). Heinemann, Viking. Edited by Vivian de Sola Pinto and Warren Roberts. Two volumes.
Selected Poems (1959). Compass. With an introduction by Kenneth Rexroth.

Plays

The Complete Plays (1965). Heinemann, Viking (1966).

Essays and Criticism

Studies in Classic American Literature (1923). Heinemann, Compass.
Selected Literary Criticism, (1956). Viking, Compass. Edited by Anthony Beal.
Phoenix (1936). Heinemann, Viking.
Phoenix II (1968). Heinemann, Viking.
Selected Essays (1950). Penguin.
Sex, Literature, and Censorship (1953). Twayne, Heinmann, Compass. Edited by Harry Moore.

Letters

The Collected Letters (1962). Heinemann, Viking. Edited by Harry Moore. Two volumes.
The Letters (1932). Heinemann, Viking. Edited by Aldous Huxley.
Letters to Bertrand Russell (1948). Gotham Book Mart. Edited by Harry Moore.
Lawrence in Love (1968). Nottingham University Press. Edited by J. T. Boulton.
The Quest for Rananim (1970). McGill-Queens University Press. Edited by George Zytaruk.
The Centaur Letters (1970). University of Texas Press.
The Selected Letters (1961). Anchor. Edited by Diana Trilling.
Selected Letters (1950). Penguin.
Letters to Martin Secker, 1911–1930 (1970). Privately printed, London.

BIOGRAPHICAL AND CRITICAL WORKS

Aldington, Richard. *D. H. Lawrence.* London: Chatto and Windus, 1930.
D. H. Lawrence: Portrait of a Genius, But. . . . New York: Duell, Sloan, and Pearce, 1950.
Arnold, Armin. *D. H. Lawrence and America.* London: The Linden Press, 1958.
Beal, Anthony. *D. H. Lawrence.* Edinburgh: Oliver and Boyd, 1961.
Boadella, David. *The Spiral Flame.* Nottingham: Ritter Press, 1956.
Brett, Dorothy. *Lawrence and Brett: A Friendship.* Philadelphia: Lippincott, 1933.
Brewster, Earl, and Brewster, Achsah. *D. H. Lawrence. Reminiscences and Correspondence.* London: Secker, 1934.
Bynner, Witter. *Journey With Genius.* New York: John Day, 1951.
Carswell, Catherine. *The Savage Pilgrimage.* New York: Harcourt, Brace, 1932 (revised edition, London: Secker, 1951).
Carter, Frederick. *The Dragon of Revelation.* London: Harmsworth, 1931.
———. *D. H. Lawrence and the Body Mystical.* London: Denis Archer, 1932.
Cavitch, David. *D. H. Lawrence and the New World.* New York: Oxford University Press, 1969.

Clark, L. D. *Dark Night of the Body.* Austin: University of Texas Press, 1964.

Clarke, Colin. *River of Dissolution.* London: Routledge and Kegan Paul, 1969.

Corke, Helen. *D. H. Lawrence: The Croyden Years.* Austin: University of Texas Press, 1965.

Daleski, Herman. *The Forked Flame: A Study of D. H. Lawrence.* Evanston: Northwestern University Press, 1965.

Delavenay, Emile. *D. H. Lawrence: The Man and His Work.* Carbondale and Edwardsville: Southern Illinois University, 1972.

Drain, Richard. *Tradition and D. H. Lawrence.* Goningen, 1960.

Draper, Ronald. *D. H. Lawrence.* New York: Twayne, 1964.

———. *D. H. Lawrence.* New York: Humanities Press, 1969.

Ford, George. *Double Measure: A Study of the Novels and Short Stories of D. H. Lawrence.* New York: Holt, Rinehart, and Winston, 1965.

Freeman, Mary. *D. H. Lawrence: A Basic Study of His Ideas.* Gainsville: University of Florida Press, 1955.

Gilbert, Sandra. *Acts of Attention.* Ithaca, N.Y., and London: Cornell University Press, 1972.

Goodheart, Eugene. *The Utopian Vison of D. H. Lawrence.* Chicago: University of Chicago Press, 1963.

Goodman, Richard. *Footnote to Lawrence.* London: The White Owl Press, 1932.

Gordon, David. *D. H. Lawrence as Literary Critic.* New Haven: Yale University Press, 1966.

Gregory, Horace. *Pilgrim of the Apocalypse.* New York: Viking Press, 1933.

Hough, Graham. *The Dark Sun: A Study of D. H. Lawrence.* New York: The Macmillan Company, 1957.

Joost, Nicholas, and Sullivan, Alvin. *D. H. Lawrence and The Dial.* Carbondale: Southern Illinois University Press, 1970.

Kenmare, Dallas (pseud.). *Fire-bird: A Study of D. H. Lawrence.* London: Barrie, 1951.

Kingsmill, Hugh. *The Life of D. H. Lawrence.* New York: Dodge Publishing, 1938.

Lawrence, Ada, and Gelder, G. Stuart. *Young Lorenzo: The Early Life of D. H. Lawrence.* London: Secker, 1932.

Lawrence, Frieda. *The Memoirs and Correspondence.* Edited by E. W. Tedlock. London: Heineman, 1961.

———. *"Not I, But the Wind. . . ."* New York: Viking, 1934.

Leavis, F. R. *D. H. Lawrence.* Cambridge: Minority Press, 1930.

————. *D. H. Lawrence, Novelist.* New York: Alfred Knopf, 1956.

Levy, Mervyn, ed. *The Paintings of D. H. Lawrence.* New York: Viking, 1964.

Luhan, Mabel Dodge. *Lorenzo in Taos.* New York: Alfred Knopf, 1932.

Merrild, Knud. *A Poet and Two Painters.* London: Routledge, 1938.

Moore, Harry. *D. H. Lawrence: His Life and Works.* Revised edition. New York: Twayne, 1964.

————. *The Intelligent Heart.* Revised edition. Baltimore: Penguin, 1960.

————. *Poste Restante: A Lawrence Travel Calendar.* With an Introduction by Mark Schorer. Berkeley: University of California Press, 1956.

————, ed. *A D. H. Lawrence Miscellany.* Carbondale: Southern Illinois University Press, 1959.

Moore, Harry, and Hoffman, Frederick, eds. *The Achievement of D. H. Lawrence.* Norman: University of Oklahoma Press, 1953.

Moore, Harry, and Roberts, Warren. *D. H. Lawrence and His World.* New York: Viking, 1966.

Moynahan, Julian. *The Deed of Life: The Novels and Tales of D. H. Lawrence.* Princeton: Princeton University Press, 1963.

Murry, J. Middleton. *Son of Woman.* New York: Cape and Smith, 1931.

————. *Reminiscenses of D. H. Lawrence.* London: Jonathan Cape, 1953.

Nehls, Edward, ed. *D. H. Lawrence: A Composite Biography.* 3 vols. Madison: University of Wisconsin Press, 1957–59.

Nin, Anäis. *D. H. Lawrence: An Unprofessional Study.* Paris: E. W. Titus, 1932.

Panichas, George. *Adventures in Consciousness: The Meaning of D. H. Lawrence's Religious Quest.* The Hague: Mouton, 1964.

Pinto, Vivian de Sola. *D. H. Lawrence: Prophet of the Midlands.* Nottingham: University of Nottingham Press, 1951.

————, ed. *D. H. Lawrence After Thirty Years, 1930–1960.* Nottingham: Curwen Press, 1960.

Powell, Lawrence Clark. *The Manuscripts of D. H. Lawrence.* Los Angeles: Public Library, 1937.

Pritchard. R. E. *D. H. Lawrence: Body of Darkness.* London: Hutchinson; University of Pittsburgh Press, 1971.

Rees, Richard. *Brave Men: A Study of D. H. Lawrence and Simone Weil.* London: Gollancz, 1958.

Roberts, Warren. *A Bibliography of D. H. Lawrence.* London: Rupert Hart-Davis, 1963.

Rolph, C. H., ed., *The Trial of Lady Chatterley.* Baltimore: Penguin Books, 1961.

Sagar, Keith. *The Art of D. H. Lawrence.* Cambridge: Cambridge University Press, 1966.

Salgado, Gamini. *D. H. Lawrence: Sons and Lovers.* London, Edward Arnold, 1966.

Schorer, Mark. *D. H. Lawrence.* New York: Dell (Laurel), 1968.

Seligman, H. J. *D. H. Lawrence: An American Interpretation.* New York: Seltzer, 1924.

Sinzell, Claude. *The Geographical Background of the Early Works of D. H. Lawrence.* Paris: Didier, 1964.

Slade, Tony. *D. H. Lawrence.* London, Evans Bros., 1969; New York, Arco, 1970.

Spilka, Mark. *The Love Ethic of D. H. Lawrence.* Bloomington: University of Indiana Press, 1955.

———, ed. *D. H. Lawrence: A Collection of Critical Essays.* Englewood Cliffs, N.J.: Prentice-Hall, 1963.

T. E. (Jessie Chambers). *D. H. Lawrence: A Personal Record.* London: Jonathan Cape, 1935.

Tedlock, E. W. *D. H. Lawrence: Artist and Rebel.* Albuquerque: University of New Mexico Press, 1963.

———, ed. *The Frieda Lawrence Collection of D. H. Lawrence Manuscripts.* Albuquerque: University of New Mexico Press, 1948.

———, ed. *D. H. Lawrence and "Sons and Lovers".* New York: New York University Press, 1965.

Tindall, William York. *D. H. Lawrence and Susan His Cow.* New York: Columbia University Press, 1939.

Tiverton, Father (Martin Jarrett-Kerr). *D. H. Lawrence and Human Existence.* London: Rockcliffe Publishing, 1951.

Vivas, Eliseo. *D. H. Lawrence: The Failure and the Triumph of Art.* Evanston: Northwestern University Press, 1960.

Weiss, Daniel. *Oedipus in Nottingham: D. H. Lawrence.* Seattle: University of Washington Press, 1962.

West, Anthony. *D. H. Lawrence.* London: Barker, 1951.

West, Rebecca. *D. H. Lawrence.* London: Secker, 1930.

White, William. *D. H. Lawrence: A Checklist of Writings, 1931–50.* Detroit: Wayne State University Press, 1950.

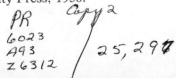

Widmer, Kingsley. *The Art of Perversity: D. H. Lawrence's Shorter Fiction.* Seattle: University of Washington Press, 1962.

Winter, Ella. *D. H. Lawrence.* Carmel, California: The Carmelite, 1930.

Young, Kenneth. *D. H. Lawrence.* New York: Longmans Green, 1951.

Yudhishtar. *Conflict in the Novels of D. H. Lawrence.* Edinburgh: Oliver and Boyd, 1969.